• • •

FIVE LADIES AND
A FORKLIFT

Thank you
for your support!

Judy Bannon

• • •

FIVE LADIES AND A FORKLIFT

Cribs for Kids' Quest to Help Every Baby Sleep Safer

JUDY BANNON
As told to Jennifer Bannon

ISBN: 1517662788
ISBN 13: 9781517662783
Library of Congress Control Number: 2015916464
CreateSpace Independent Publishing Platform
North Charleston, South Carolina

*This book is dedicated to our Cribs for Kids partners
and all of the babies and families they tirelessly serve.*

CONTENTS

PROLOGUE

Eighty percent of success is showing up.

—*Woody Allen*

I can trace the beginning of my nonprofit career back to a volunteer shift I never signed up for. It was 1985. I was a thirty-nine-year-old mother of three working as a legal secretary at a law firm in Downtown Pittsburgh. I'd had various jobs over the years but nothing I could call a career, and while I'd always been fascinated with the law, I knew this job was more a practical measure than a new direction in life. Our country was changing, and two-income households were becoming the norm. With our Irish twins, Sean and Kelly, both scheduled to enter college within two years, my husband, Dick, and I thought it was a smart time for me to get back in the workforce. I enjoyed my days—riding the train to and from our suburb-of-a-suburb of Pittsburgh with a colorful group of neighbors, learning the ins and outs of the cases the firm was working on as I typed dictation and overheard conversations in the break room, and purposefully bustling around the city at lunchtime in a skirt and sneakers. I secretly toyed with the idea of going to law school, but we had three kids to put through college before I could dream of going back. I suppose I was searching for my life's work, even if I didn't realize it. So I worked hard at my job, and I always said yes when new experiences came my way.

One day Michaelleene Conley, my friend since she'd been my model attendant when I sold real estate for Ryan Homes in the late '70s, called me with an opportunity. Well, I suppose it was a favor, but someone once told me those two things aren't mutually exclusive. It seemed she had volunteered to work a shift answering phones at the United Cerebral Palsy telethon that weekend, but something had come up. Maybe I could fill in for her? It sounded kind of fun—being behind the scenes at a TV station, maybe getting to see some local celebrities. Plus, I'd always had a hard time leaving work undone. I said yes and made a quick decision to enlist my daughter Kelly's majorette troupe to join me, figuring it was a win-win. The girls would get volunteer experience, and the telethon would get a group of fresh, young people whose main passion was talking on the phone for hours.

The telethon took place over a January weekend. It was snowing as I drove around the township picking up baton twirlers who ran out to the car with heads down to keep their perfectly curled bangs in place, shrieking and giggling as they jumped into my K-car. They spent the whole ride to the TV station talking a mile a minute about algebra, boys and leotards. I tried my best to tune out their conversation, never eager to know *too* much about the private lives of other people's teenage daughters.

When we arrived at the studio, we were greeted by… no one. It seemed that not only had my friend not been able to show up for her shift, but the person in charge of this twenty-one-hour-long, live-televised event had also neglected to show up, or perhaps had disappeared somewhere along the way. After almost an hour of waiting around for direction, I started into a mild panic. It was snowing outside—rather heavily at this point. I'd pulled all these young women away from the comfort and safety of their homes twenty miles away on a Sunday afternoon with the purpose of doing some good for the community. I figured I'd better quickly find something productive for them to do. Looking around, I noticed the phone bank was mostly empty, so I began to assign the girls to stations, trying to keep in mind who was a leader, who was a follower, and who had just stolen whose boyfriend. Scrambling around, I found a pile of papers that seemed to explain what one should do upon answering the phone, so I passed those out and explained the procedure to my charges, noticing that the volunteers who'd already been on the phones for a while seemed grateful to finally receive some direction as well.

Pretty soon, things really started to hum. My girls were smoothly answering the phones and taking donations, and I had a group of volunteers waiting in the wings to spell them off when they needed a break. I had someone running drinks and other refreshments back and forth to the on-screen talent, and I was tallying up figures for the big tote-board reveal at the top of the hour.

I only had one problem. People seemed to think that I was in charge. I'd never had a shortage of common sense, so I was able to come up with reasonable answers to most of the questions that floated my way, but I wasn't sure what the endgame was. What was going to happen when someone who actually was in charge wandered in? Would I be seen as a savior or a usurper? I figured I would just keep my head down and keep things afloat the best I could.

After running the volunteer pool for a couple of hours, I was approached by a distinguished-looking, white-haired gentleman.

"Excuse me, ma'am. What is your name?" he asked me.

"I'm Judy Bannon," I replied, wondering if I should have cooked up an alias. Could this be a trap? Could you be arrested for hijacking a telethon?

"How did you come to be in charge of this?"

"Oh, I'm not in charge. I'm just a volunteer," I answered.

"Yes, I understand that. I guess I'm in charge ultimately, although one of my employees is supposed to be doing the job that you've taken on so admirably."

"Oh." I wasn't sure where to go with that. Was he angry with me? Had I overstepped my boundaries?

"I'm wondering if you could get me your résumé," he continued. I felt like I'd just been pulled over for speeding and was being asked for license and registration. How far would a big smile and a wink get me in this situation?

"You mean, right now?"

"No"—he paused briefly—"what I'm saying is that you're doing a lovely job in the absence of anyone who works for me doing their job, so I'm hoping you might send me your résumé this week. I'd like to consider you for a job in the future. We're going to be looking to add some people to our development department."

Is this guy serious, or is he using me to prove a point to his employees? I was uncertain but flattered nevertheless. I worked double time for the rest of the afternoon with his business card burning a hole in my pocket. As I dropped off the girls in reverse order through the varied and snow-covered neighborhoods of Elizabeth Township later, I pictured the possibilities—my duties, my salary, my office. It wasn't until I went home and shared the news with Dick that I started to worry I might be in over my head.

What exactly was I going to put on my résumé that would sound even remotely like something that would qualify me to work for this man? More importantly, what exactly did one do in a development department? It must have something to do with fund-raising, right? We'd been at a telethon, after all. I lay in bed that night and searched my memory for anything I'd done that could qualify as fund-raising. Right before I dropped off into sleep, I had a eureka moment. The PTA! I'd been president when my two oldest kids were in elementary school. That had been all about raising money. Visions of renting bounce houses and spin-art machines for the Spring Fling and transforming the art classroom into a Santa's Secret Shop bombarded me. Roller-skating parties and hoagie sales took on the stature of great marketing campaigns as I hung my hopes on them as proof of my worth.

The next evening when I got home from work, I sat down in the laundry room at the family typewriter, under the clothesline hung with children's snowsuits and 1970s maternity clothes, and updated my résumé to reflect my days in development at Mount Vernon Elementary School. I still felt a little sheepish, but before I could think better of it, I slid the crisp sheet of bond paper into a manila envelope and sent it off.

• • •

I was so worried about proving myself on that sheet of paper, trying to think of the magic turns of phrase that would make me seem like everything Mr. Enck was looking for in an employee. What I didn't understand was that I had already proven myself. Just as I'd tucked away his business card in the secret spot in my wallet, he'd tucked away the memory of me taking charge of an event in which I had no responsibility or vested interest. Even though I might not have had ten years' experience in marketing and fund-raising, I had the instinct to say yes to new opportunities and the work ethic to dig in when a job needed to be done—qualities that would serve me throughout the rest of my career.

It's hard to imagine what my life would be today—what career (or string of jobs) I would have fallen into—if I hadn't shown up at that telethon. A few months later he called as promised, and I began working in development at United Cerebral Palsy, which led to another opportunity as executive director of the Greater

Pittsburgh Chapter of the National SIDS Foundation in 1989, where nine years later I created the Cribs for Kids Campaign with two employees working out of a couple of shoebox-sized offices that had once been dorm rooms for student nurses at a neighborhood hospital. Since that time we've put over three hundred thousand babies into safe-sleep environments; traveled the world to educate physicians, advocates, and parents; lobbied local, state, and federal governments to pass legislation requiring safe-sleep education to new mothers; and grown to include more than six hundred fifty partners in all fifty states and the United States Commonwealth of Saipan.

Over the past five years, I've shared the story of Cribs for Kids with thousands of people and have been told again and again, "You should write a book." (I hope they really meant it!) At first I laughed it off, but as you'll learn, I don't shrink easily from a challenge. So I started to ask myself, *What would the purpose of this book be?* My first thought was that it could be a how-to book. After all, we'd managed to take Cribs for Kids from an idea to a nonprofit with a $4,700,000 budget in less than a decade. We were in a unique position, though, in that we had a product—the Graco Pack 'n Play—to sell. Most nonprofits would not be able to follow that model. Next I considered telling the story of my career, but as the movie *The Aviator* taught us a few years back, even the life of Howard Hughes can be boring if you try to tell it as a story, and he was a famously eccentric hermit who dated Katherine Hepburn. The problem is that life doesn't have a plot.

So I asked myself and the women who made up my team at that time—Eileen, Barb, Heather, and Paulette (the Five Ladies)—what it is that keeps us inspired each day? What is the magic ingredient that makes Cribs for Kids not just a successful venture but a story that people feel needs to be told? When we began to discuss it, we always came back to the same answer: the hand of God. Initially, I think I resisted that answer because I don't want this book to turn off people of different faiths or no faith or still-discovering faith. So if the word *God* doesn't work for you, think instead *universe* or *fate or Goddess*. Whatever you want to call it, there is a driving force that has kept us going when we were frustrated or clueless or intimidated or just plain scared, signs along the way that have encouraged us to keep going and let us know that we were on the right path. By following these signs, we've created something bigger than ourselves, something that has moved beyond our small team and our modest city to better the lives of people all over the world.

This book is the story of how we did that and the lessons we learned along the way. In order to avoid the pedantic nature of the how-to book, or the meandering qualities of a professional biography, I've split this book into ten sections, centering each around a lesson or a belief that has shaped our vision and our work. Hopefully these lessons will be meaningful to you, either personally or professionally, and if we're all lucky, you'll get a few laughs along the way. (If you don't, I'm not telling the story correctly.)

All right, let's get started. Thanks for showing up.

Lesson 1

●　●　●

THERE ARE NO SHORTCUTS ON YOUR PATH.

Leap and the net will appear.

—John Burroughs

It was four years later, the day after a different United Cerebral Palsy Telethon, when my life took another fateful turn. I was at the Channel 4 studios wrapping up loose ends, exhausted but glowing from the grueling twenty-one-hour event that had brought in more than $22 million nationwide. In Pittsburgh we'd raised over $500,000, the largest amount in our chapter's history. I was in the studio gathering up clipboards, scripts, and dirty coffee cups, chatting with Joe Denardo, the station's meteorologist and host of the telethon, when a voice came over the PA. "Judy, Ray Mansfield is on the phone for you."

Who's Ray Mansfield, and why is he calling me here? Joe looked at me curiously. I shrugged my shoulders and waved off the call. With my head full of spinning tote boards and hands full of crumpled scripts, answering a cold call was the last thing on my agenda.

"Um, can you take a number and tell him I'll call him back, please?"

A moment later a receptionist walked into the room and handed me a pink slip of paper. *It's very important I talk to you. Please call at your earliest convenience.* I folded the paper, put it in my coat pocket, and forgot about it.

When I got back to UCP, Michaelleene was in our shared office amid a pile of notes detailing the highlights of the telethon and what could be improved for next year. (When I was promoted to development director, I had hired her knowing I could depend on her to work hard and keep me laughing each day.) She looked up from her desk and said, "Someone named Ray Mansfield called for you."

"He called the studio, too. Did he say why he was calling?"

"Not sure. I just saw the message on your desk. Who is he?"

"I have no idea," I said.

"He called the studio? That's kind of weird. What time?"

"About eleven, I guess."

"I think he called here this morning and then again at around three thirty," she told me.

I was curious but exhausted. *I'll call him from home*, I figured, remembering that I had his number in my pocket. Of course, at home, dinner distracted me when I walked in the door. I managed to stay awake as I stirred the spaghetti sauce; the oven timer broke me out of a trance before the garlic bread burned. I didn't even remember getting into bed, but next thing I knew, I was waking up there at 7:00 a.m. Needless to say, I didn't think about the mysterious phone calls again until I was driving to work later that day.

Ray Mansfield was the name of the Steelers' center from the mid-1960s through the mid-1970s, so it makes sense that it was while listening to sports highlights on the radio that it hit me. *Crap, I forgot to call that guy!* By the time I got to the office, he'd already called once and left a message with the answering service. *Give him points for persistence.* After grabbing a cup of coffee, I called back, ending the suspense for both of us.

"Hello, this is Judy Bannon. I've received several messages that you're trying to contact me."

"Hi, Judy! It's great to hear from you! You're probably wondering what this is all about."

"Actually, yes. I was trying to remember if we've ever met, but the only Ray Mansfield I've heard of is the Steeler," I joked.

"Oh…well, that's me. Are you a football fan?"

My jaw dropped. Dick and I had had season tickets since the early '70s and had been fortunate enough to attend every home game throughout the Steel Curtain years, even traveling with our friends to away games in Cleveland and Cincinnati in a rented Winnebago, proudly sporting our black-and-gold "Only a Steeler fan would weekend in Ohio" gear we'd had made at a local T-shirt shop. When we were stuck watching away games on TV, we often shouted so loudly at the screen that my youngest daughter, Jennie, would rush into the room and shush us in a classic parent-child reversal. "The whole neighborhood can hear you!" she'd say. (Which wasn't actually true, because the whole neighborhood was screaming at their own TV sets. Such is the way of football in Pittsburgh.)

"Sure, who isn't around here?" I answered, trying to be cool. "So what can I help you with, Mr. Mansfield?"

"Oh, please, call me Ray." Ray! I couldn't wait to tell Dick about this. "Judy, I'm on the board of the Western Pennsylvania Chapter of the National SIDS Foundation. We raise money to fund research on sudden infant death syndrome, or SIDS. We also provide support services to grieving parents. Are you familiar with SIDS?"

"I think so. Is that crib death?" I asked.

"Yes, many people still know it by that name, although SIDS is the preferred term these days. I was watching your telethon this weekend and was so impressed by the amount of money that you raised. I'd love for you to come work for us." A job offer? That was the last thing I had expected.

"Oh, Mr. Mansfield, Ray, thank you, but I'm devoted to our cause at UCP."

"I'm sure you are. It's an important cause. I've been wondering, how many babies are affected by cerebral palsy each year?"

"About forty-two hundred."

"Forty-two hundred, I see. And the national telethon this weekend raised twenty-two million. That's great. Did you know that seven to ten thousand babies die each year of SIDS, and no one knows why? They're perfectly healthy one minute and gone the next, never make it to their first birthdays, yet on an annual basis we barely raise one tenth of what UCP raised this past weekend."

I was shocked by those numbers. It didn't seem possible. I asked him to tell me more. "Well, there are many challenges that we face when it comes to raising money. One is that SIDS has been a mystery for so long. We've never had the big 'aha!' research moment. There are some theories about the cause, but we're still largely in the dark. Continuing to put money into research strikes many donors as fruitless. As far as raising money from the public, well, people just don't want to talk about it or even *think* about it. Perfectly healthy babies dying for no reason and no preventive measures to offer? It's a tough sell. It's the kind of story people turn away from, unless they have a personal connection, of course."

I asked if he had a personal connection, and he told me about his business partner and close friend, Chuck Puskar, who'd lost his son Bryan to SIDS in 1976. Bryan had been Ray's godson. Although it had been almost fifteen years since he'd passed, Ray told me he could remember that phone call like it was yesterday. We all struggle with what to say, how to help loved ones who are grieving. Ray helped by throwing himself into fundraising. He inspired the Pittsburgh Chapter of the NFL Alumni Association to adopt SIDS as one of its causes, garnering donations from their charitable events and creating the annual Legends of Pro Football banquet, which was the most lucrative fund raiser the chapter held. He was grateful that his status as a gridiron legend in a football-crazy town could inspire people to give. It turned out that I was as susceptible to those pleas as anyone.

"Our board has formed a search committee to hire an executive director. I think someone with your fundraising expertise could be what we're looking for. We simply have to raise more money for research if we're going to put an end to this tragedy."

I was moved by the story and statistics he'd shared with me. However, he'd also said that his organization only had $13,000 in the bank. ("That's why we need you!" he told me.) That wouldn't even cover my salary. With two kids in college, I couldn't make a hasty decision. Ray was so passionate, though, that I found myself having a hard time saying no. I asked for some time to think about it.

I didn't know, couldn't even imagine, the pain of losing a child, but I do know the pain of having three miscarriages and of losing a loved one too early and without explanation. I was thirty years old in 1975 when my beautiful baby brother, Danny, died in the night at age twenty-two. Initially it was speculated that he'd had a heart attack, but he'd had no history of heart problems. How does a healthy young man die in bed of a heart attack, anyway? Dr. Cyril Wecht, the well-known medical examiner and coroner of Allegheny County who'd become famous consulting on a number of high-profile deaths, including John and Robert Kennedy, performed the autopsy and came away from it flummoxed. I remember the shock of realizing that even this brilliant, celebrated doctor couldn't give my family any answers for why we'd lost our dear brother, my mother's baby boy.

I knew I had no business leaving a job at an established nonprofit to work at this more fledgling organization. I couldn't get Danny out of my mind though. As I researched SIDS, I was struck by the speculation of Dr. Marie Valdez-Dapena, who believed that there was a connection between Sudden Cardiac Death (a sudden, unexpected death caused by loss of heart function) and SIDS. It began to feel more and more like something I had to do, no longer a choice but an imperative. If I could raise money to help solve the mystery of SIDS, maybe I would also finally learn the reason for Danny's death.

I agreed to interview for the job, and within a few weeks, I was hired. Much to my dismay, the $13,000 I thought they had in the bank was actually their budget. In reality their bank account showed a balance of a little over $2,000. I had to get to work.

For the first fifteen years or so that I worked for the SIDS cause, our offices were housed in an annex of South Side Hospital. When I started there, South Side was a working-class neighborhood scraping by after the closing of the J&L steel mill that once stood proudly at its outskirts. Our offices were located in Roesch-Taylor Hall, a building that had been constructed as a nursing-school dorm but had been converted to office space in the 1980s. The interior looked pretty much like you'd expect a college dorm to look—a central hallway with single rooms down either side, each accessed by its own door. We had two of these rooms, one for me and eventually one for Michaelleene, whom I brought on board as director of development about five months after I'd taken the job. (What can I say? We were a duo. Sometimes more Lucy and Ethel than Lennon and McCartney, but a duo nonetheless.) We spent our days standing in each other's doorways talking (or yelling through the wall when we were too busy or too tired to get up) like coeds sharing gossip or class notes. Storage consisted of large closets with sliding wooden doors and built-in dressers that were good for hanging winter coats and stockpiling office supplies, but not much else. Eventually, Ray Tasillo, brother of Eileen Carlins (who at the time was our peer-contact coordinator), built a long counter down the left side of each room, in the hot-pink and electric-blue shades of our logo, under a shelving unit that covered the whole wall to create additional work and storage space. We crammed the other side of the rooms with our secondhand teacher's desks and as many filing cabinets as we could poach from storage rooms throughout the building.

Each room had one large, west-facing window that let in the late-day sun and looked out over the colorful row houses and church steeples of the South Side slopes and flats to the bridges crossing the Monongahela River, which carried city dwellers and the suburban denizens of the South Hills to their jobs in Downtown skyscrapers. I could look down at the hospital parking lot that we used for our annual Pierogie Cook-Off fund raiser during July's South Side Summer Street Spectacular; Red and Irene's, the shot-and-a-beer bar on the corner; and the apartment that Sean and Kelly had rented from the hospital for years (sometimes separately, sometimes together).

Those offices are where Cribs for Kids was born in 1998. The first day I reported to work there, though, was as executive director of the Western Pennsylvania Chapter of the National SIDS Foundation, raising money for research, awareness, and grief counseling. Ray's friend Chuck Puskar and his wife, Jan, had started this local chapter after their son Bryan's death. They were angry and confused that so little was known about SIDS. One day, not long after losing him, they saw a PSA on television sponsored by the National SIDS Foundation and called to learn how they could get involved. Initially they worked with the national organization, of which Chuck became a trustee in 1980. Locally, they began a peer-contact network out of their home, fielding phone calls at their kitchen table from other SIDS parents and offering support in the form of conversations with people who'd been there. Eventually they set up a SIDS Management System in cooperation with the Allegheny County Coroner's Office, which provided them with contact information of all families who'd lost their babies. To the Puskars, this meant that no one in the county would fall through the cracks, suffering through the aftermath of SIDS alone. However, they wanted to do more, so in 1981, they officially started the Greater Pittsburgh Chapter of the National SIDS Foundation with a core group of parent volunteers.

Chuck and Jan's grassroots phone support grew into a strong peer-counseling network that included monthly support meetings facilitated by parents Kay Falkenhan and Karen Ebert, licensed social worker Wes Weidenhamer, and medical advisor Dr. Keith Reisinger. Additionally, the chapter held gatherings, like an annual summer picnic, so families could get to know one another in less intense social settings. They became active in fund-raising, with their most lucrative events resulting from Ray's involvement with the NFL Alumni.

Another key part of the chapter's services was providing SIDS education to local hospitals, coroners, public-health nurses, police, EMTs, and funeral directors. In those days many parents were met with suspicion or outright hostility by first responders and hospital staff who, knowing little about SIDS, assumed that foul play was involved in their babies' deaths. This education was crucial to helping these professionals understand what a SIDS death looked like so that they could provide appropriate support to parents at that dark hour. It also helped raise awareness of the chapter, which enabled the peer-contact network to set a goal of reaching all local parents within forty-eight hours of their child's death.

A quarterly newsletter, *The Loose Leaf* (this name came from the logo for the National SIDS Foundation that depicted a tree representing the family and a fallen leaf for the child who had died), reported on research findings and chapter activities; published inspirational and instructive advice for dealing with grief, as well as poetry and other personal tributes written by parents; and kept the chapter connected to its supporters.

I spent my first week on the job poring through binders filled with back issues of the newsletter and consuming all of the literature the national organization had published over the past decade. I had a lot to learn about the syndrome and the SIDS community: who were the major players in research, fund-raising, and counseling? I also called each of the board members and introduced myself, asking them what had drawn them to the cause, how long they'd been on the board, and what their hopes for the organization were. I most looked forward to speaking with Jim Agras, president of Triangle Tech, a network of Pennsylvania-based career-education schools. He was a major force in the philanthropic and business communities in Pittsburgh, one of those people whom everyone knows and respects. Truthfully, his presence on the board was one of the reasons I felt comfortable accepting the job. I knew that having him as an ally could open a lot of doors. It also signaled to me that the chapter, while small, was seen as a viable entity.

When I called him, we made small talk for a few minutes. Then he said, "Well, Judy, I'm so glad that you accepted the job. It sounds like you have a great head on your shoulders."

I was beaming. "Thank you."

"It makes me feel better about what I'm about to say. I'm afraid I'm going to have to resign my position on the board."

The warm, fuzzy feeling that had been building inside me throughout the call evaporated instantly.

"You can't!" I blurted before I could stop myself.

"My responsibilities at Triangle Tech are increasing, and I feel like I'm not able to devote as much time to SIDS as I'd like. It doesn't seem fair to you or the organization."

"Please, don't even worry about that. You can devote as much or as little time as you like. In fact, you don't even have to come to the meetings. But we need you on this board. *I* need you. You're one of the main reasons I took this job."

"Oh, well, that's nice of you to say, but…"

"No, I mean it. Having your name and experience behind us is invaluable. We need money desperately, and having a strong board makes such a difference when dealing with foundations and writing grants.

Please, just give me six months," I told him, knowing that if we didn't make some money to keep us afloat, I probably wouldn't be around by then anyway. He acquiesced, agreeing to send his executive assistant, Vickie Bentley, to attend meetings when he couldn't. (Vickie became a vital member of the board and a close friend of mine until her untimely death in 2013.) When I hung up the phone, I was slightly embarrassed that I hadn't had the grace to accept his resignation, wondering if I'd made the right move or rubbed him the wrong way. That interaction taught me a valuable lesson about speaking up and asking for what you need. So much of running a nonprofit is just that—finding people who are willing to help. You'll never find them if you don't speak up. As my friend Bonnie DiCarlo says, "If you don't ask, they can't say yes."

Jim Agras has stuck with us to this day as a current board member of Cribs for Kids, and more than once it's been his influence and connections that have kept us from closing our doors.

I had taken on a big job and wasn't interested in reinventing the wheel. The grief-support services the chapter offered were already a success, so after approaching Noreen Crowell (my friend since fourth grade and current board member) and her stepmother, Meg Dougherty, to donate the services of Meg-a-Phone, their twenty-four-hour answering service, assuring parents could receive support within minutes at any time of the day or night, I focused my efforts on fund-raising. In addition to a full calendar of fund-raising events every year at UCP, each telethon had been like nonprofit grad school—coordinating and training volunteers; handling on-screen talent; writing engaging, fact-filled scripts peppered with new and inventive ways to ask for donations; soliciting in-kind donations for around-the-clock food and drink—all on live TV.

Naturally we continued the annual Legends of Pro Football Banquet, which, aside from raising a ton of money, was always a thrilling evening. How could you go wrong with a roster of football legends like Ray Mansfield, Mike Webster, Jack Lambert, Jack Ham, Rocky Bleier, Franco Harris, Andy Russell, and Lynn Swann playing host as they dined with the guests at tables throughout the ballroom? The only thing better than being a guest at the banquet was attending the VIP reception in the Presidential Suite of the hotel, where guests could mingle with local newscasters and celebrities and buy footballs and other memorabilia that their favorite players would sign.

I was able to carry over one of my most successful fund raisers from UCP. In celebration of Secretary's Day (back when that title was preferred to administrative assistant), we sold Tribute to Secretaries canvas gift bags emblazoned with our logo and filled with coupons for free merchandise and services from local restaurants, salons, stores, sightseeing tours, theater tickets, and the like, as well as candy, soda, and makeup samples. Of course, since the traditional Secretary's Day gift was flowers, each bag was adorned with a fresh carnation. Not so long removed from the *Mad Men* days, in the eighties many male bosses were still in the habit of sending their (usually) female secretaries shopping whenever they needed gifts for the women in their lives, so needing a gift for one's secretary was a conundrum. One thousand bags at twenty-five dollars each sold out every year. We enlisted the help of volunteers to assemble the gift bags. Many of our volunteers had retired from United States Steel Corporation, Bell Telephone, and Westinghouse Corporation. They brought with them energy and professionalism that added to the success of this project. The South Side Hospital offered their conference room, which we turned into our assembly line.

That was the easy part, however. The countless letters and phone calls soliciting donations, designing and printing coupons, and finding clever ways to spread the word to bosses took months. In the lead-up to Secretary's Day, Michaelleene and I were in constant motion, schlepping bags up and down elevators and in and out of our cars to the pickup stations we'd created Downtown, manned by our trusty volunteers. We even personally delivered bags to businesses outside the city. Since all the contents were donated by local businesses, the proceeds were pure profit. Twenty-five thousand dollars was a huge take for us, and we were willing to work for it.

Another successful and labor-intensive fund raiser each year was our Christmas Gift Wrap. What started out as one booth at Century III Mall, a mammoth three-story '80s dream mall with four anchor stores, grew over ten or twelve years to include multiple booths throughout that mall and others around the city (including a booth at the Air Mall at Pittsburgh International Airport that we had to shutter after 9/11 when we were informed we couldn't have scissors in the areas beyond the X-ray machines). The malls donated the space to us, as well as tables, chairs, wrapping paper, bows, gift tags, tape, scissors, and so on.

The booths operated from the day after Thanksgiving through Christmas Eve. Knowing that everyone was enticed by the F word (free), we adorned the booths with signs that read "Free Gift Wrap." Of course, when they got up to the counter, customers were greeted by smiling volunteers wearing pins that announced "I am a SIDS Volunteer—Thank You for Your Donation" and a huge fishbowl stuffed with money. We coordinated our volunteers for three four-hour shifts each day. When holiday commitments or snowstorms kept them away, staffmembers worked overtime. Aside from Michaelleene, me, and our kids, Eileen Carlins and her family were regular wrappers. Eileen and her husband, Dan, had lost their daughter, Rachel, to SIDS in 1980. They were regular attendees at our monthly support meetings, and Eileen was on call twenty-four-hours-a-day as a peer contact for grieving parents. Dan has long been active in the cause too. For years he was our treasurer and continues to serve as one of our most dependable and devoted board members. Eileen's kids, Matt, Sarah, and Emily, remember wondering every year if they would be deemed grown enough to graduate to wrapping presents or if they would end up spending another season sitting under the counter making pull-apart bows. Her daughter Sarah was small for her age. At ten she was promoted to the rank of wrapper, but she had to stand on a chair while she worked. One customer was so happy with her handiwork that he wanted to give her her own gift.

"How old are you?" he asked.

"I'm ten," she answered.

"Well, here's ten dollars for the donation bowl and a ten-dollar tip for you," he said, handing her a crisp bill. Without a thought, she put her tip into the bowl, too, knowing this labor of love was in memory of her sister Rachel.

In early December, I had some time throughout the day to knit or write grants longhand on pads of legal paper (no laptops back then) as I leaned on the front counter of the booth, humming along with the piped-in holiday music that still sounded fresh to my ears. As Christmas drew nearer, however, mania set in. We found ourselves catering to a constant line of bleary-eyed customers weighted down with endless bags full of gifts, that infernal Christmas music on its thousandth loop, so expert at eyeballing the precise amount of paper needed to cover a sweater box that we sometimes wanted to shout for joy and approval, "Look at this! Not a square inch to spare!" By December 15 we could barely remember a meal that didn't come from the food court, and the muscles in our hands had grown strong enough to strangle Rudolph. Looking back, I have no idea how I ever got Christmas ready for my family in those days, as I often left for work at 8:00 a.m. and didn't get home until 10:00 p.m. Of course, the booth was a great place to get gift ideas, so that helped. I'd see something I thought Dick would like, for instance, ask the customer where he or she got it, buy it during my next break, and wrap it during a lull later in the evening.

Certain years still stand out—the year Starbucks mercifully found its way to the malls; the time someone asked me with a straight face to wrap a beanbag chair, and I did it; the year a man offered us one hundred dollars five minutes before the mall closed on Christmas Eve to wrap his entire haul. "I don't care what paper you use. I don't care if they're messy. I just need them to be wrapped when I walk in the door tonight." There were four of us there that evening—Michaelleene, her daughter Erin, Jennie and me. If a representative from the *Guinness Book of World Records* had been present, we surely would have set a wrapping record, outdoing even all the parents who would be up that same night, living rooms covered in bows and scraps of scotch tape, remnants of paper being dragged through the house by dogs and cats. That was the year we wandered around the half-dark mall, the only people in the midst of all of that caged-in merchandise, like the sole survivors in a zombie-apocalypse movie, searching for anyone who could unlock the doors so we could get out to the parking lot and hightail it home. It was takeout pizza and midnight mass at our house that year, but how could I say no to a donation like that? It was almost superstition, as if saying no signaled to the universe that our coffers were forever full and would doom us to never raise another cent. I think that's the attitude you have to have, though, especially in the early years of an enterprise.

As overwhelming as daily life at the mall in December could be, it was thrilling too. We've all had those moments in our lives when money flies out of our pockets; it's the mental disassociation from one's bank account that has led to the creation of the wedding industry. Well, that's Christmas at the mall, and we were on the receiving end, donation bowls running over, getting a piece of the holiday pie for the cause. Our take each day grew so large that we'd need security to walk us to our cars, and we'd make the bank deposit before even reaching home.

In spite of its hectic nature, the gift-wrap booth was predicated on an elegantly simple exchange: we provided a needed service and were paid in cash. In the hand-to-mouth world of nonprofits, where every day is a new plea for funding, that was deeply satisfying. In the process, we raised awareness when people asked questions about SIDS as we wrapped. Sometimes we unexpectedly gave someone the opportunity to share their story—"My friend's baby died of SIDS. It was so shocking and sad." There was one man who came every year on Christmas Eve, had one small gift wrapped, and gave us a fifty-dollar bill. Though he never shared his motivation for this act, it was clear this ritual had meaning for him. Every year this fund raiser brought in over $40,000. Not bad for a *free* gift wrap.

We had many other fund raisers too—a canister campaign that had us always on the go, emptying the canisters we'd placed in banks, restaurants, and stores all over Allegheny County; United Way Donor Option; and direct mail pleas. We sold thousands of those entertainment books that were stuffed with BOGO coupons for local restaurants and attractions. We planned events like car cruises, golf outings, concerts, and a would-only-happen-in-Pittsburgh "Pierogie Cook-Off." Aside from raising much needed funds, each of these events increased awareness of SIDS in our county. Working them gave us the opportunity to see how knowledge grew. The questions changed from "What is SIDS?" to "SIDS is when babies die and no one knows why, right?" followed by questions, stories, and associations. The realization that awareness was growing bolstered us on the low days when money was scarce and support meetings were full.

Sometimes awareness was hard to come by, though. One year we worked with a local outdoor-advertising firm to have billboards donated during June promoting an upcoming fund raiser. Since it was a donation, there was no guarantee of how many billboards would be placed, where they would be, or how long they would stay up. Driving back to the office from a meeting on the North Side one day, I spotted one of our billboards along the Allegheny River in the Strip District. I was elated. I stopped at Stutz Pharmacy on Carson Street, a couple of blocks down from our offices, to buy a disposable camera, picked up Michaelleene, and headed back to take a picture for our newsletter. By the time we got back to the billboard, thirty minutes at the most, it was already removed! So much for donated advertising space. Never shrinking violets, we immediately called the ad company and complained (on what grounds, I'm not sure) and name-dropped Bob O'Connor, board member and city councilman. We managed to get the billboard put back up...for about a week. However, it was long enough to get the snapshot we wanted. Just another example of speaking up and asking for what you want.

Although the content has changed over the years as research has broadened our understanding of SIDS and other causes of infant death, education has always been a vital part of what we do. In the eighties and nineties, one of our chief aims was to educate professionals who came into contact with families of SIDS victims at the time of death. Procedures and protocols for identifying and properly handling a SIDS death, as well as sensitivity training to ensure parents were treated with dignity and respect throughout the process, often made the difference between a supportive and a scarring experience. EMTs, police officers, and even emergency-room staff that aren't familiar with SIDS can jump to conclusions about the circumstances leading to an infant's death, causing them to treat grieving, shocked parents with suspicion or hostility.

Part of our outreach involved inviting these professionals to our annual regional SIDS conferences. Throughout the rest of the year, we crisscrossed the state in my car, speaking at police trainings, medical schools, hospitals, conventions for funeral directors and coroners—any venue where we thought we could reach our target audience. At first it was intimidating, speaking to rooms full of cops and doctors, hoping to teach them something their vast experience and years of training hadn't covered. At times I could tell that my audience shared this view, checking their watches, anxious to get back to their responsibilities. When Eileen presented with me, she would always speak first, telling the story of the night Rachel died, sharing the clinical as well as the emotional details. Her courage and honesty would melt even the toughest and most jaded hearts in the room, opening them up to the knowledge that we hoped to impart.

I would sometimes become downtrodden or irritated or downright jealous over how hard we worked physically, mentally, and emotionally and how easily money seemed to flow to other charities. It always felt like those with money were given more money. (Pink ribbons, anyone?) We bled for every dollar. However, if we hadn't wrapped mountains of gifts, stuffed thousands of tote bags, educated the already highly educated, and guilted advertising firms into plastering our message around the city, what would we have learned? Grants are great, but staying holed up in your office typing eight hours a day doesn't teach you anything about your community. Nor does it teach your community anything about you.

Through the years we met thousands of people with whom we had thousands of conversations, sharing our mission and goals with them and learning about their experiences, needs, hopes, and questions. We saw firsthand how SIDS awareness rose over the years as we chatted with attendees at various events and fund raisers throughout the county. We were reminded of the importance of our mission as we met parents who shared their stories while having their gifts wrapped on cold winter days. We forged emotional connections with first responders, seeing how simple human stories can affect even those who have seemingly seen and heard it all. We learned how much this work meant to us as we pushed through exhaustion to stick around for a few extra minutes to earn a few extra dollars. At age seventy, I'm grateful to not have to drive hundreds of miles each month to speaking engagements, grabbing a couple of hours of sleep pulled over at a rest stop to save money on hotels; to not be on my feet all day wrapping gifts or handing out informational pamphlets; to not make countless cold calls to local businesses and elected officials looking for support. I would do it all again, though, relive every moment. Not because nostalgia makes romance of our toughest times, and not because I don't have it in me to take it easy—although both are true. We tend to think experiences like those lead us to our life's work, but actually they create our life's work. There is a saying, "Stars are made, not born." I think the same is true of purpose.

No one is born with a clear vision of the contribution he or she will make, and no one will find it through daydreams. Being an active participant in life, willing to do the hard work, realizing that no part of the job is beneath you, saying yes more than you say no, making phone calls that scare you, and having uncomfortable conversations—these are the steps to finding your path. Don't be afraid to walk them.

A BRIEF HISTORY OF SIDS

*Adapted from research compiled
by Dr. Eileen Tyrala*

*Those who cannot remember the past
are condemned to repeat it.*

—George Santayana

In 1992 I was asked to speak about marketing at the International SIDS Conference in Sydney, Australia. I wasn't sure what I was more proud of—the fact that I was recognized as someone with something to teach or that our chapter actually had enough money in the bank to afford a plane ticket to the other side of the world. Of course, those two occurrences weren't unrelated. Our fund-raising efforts and grant writing had increased our budget over three years to $250,000.

I've never been a big traveler, so while I was thrilled with being asked to share some of our marketing strategies, I have to admit that my thoughts after the initial thrill were not of the Sydney Opera House or Bondi Beach or even Crocodile Dundee. All I could think was, "Does it really take a whole day to fly there?" Before my jet lag had worn off, though, I realized that if ever there was an event at which to show up, this was it.

The first-day plenary was presented by Kaarene Fitzgerald, head of the Australian SIDS Alliance, and Ed Mitchell, who had spent the past three years researching why Australia, the United Kingdom, and New Zealand had the highest rates of SIDS in the world, averaging 2.1 deaths per one thousand live births, compared to Japan with the lowest rates, only .3 deaths per one thousand. (The United States' rates were 1.3 per thousand at that time.) What was Japan doing differently? What were the variables? Mitchell decided it had to be connected to how the different cultures were laying their babies down to sleep. Japanese infants were put to sleep on their backs on tatami mats, while babies in the UK, Australia, and New Zealand were often placed on their stomachs in sheepskin bedding. That first day at the conference, much to our amazement and delight,

Mitchell and Fitzgerald presented a simple remedy: laying babies on their backs to sleep. That simple change had helped them slash SIDS rates in the UK, Australia, and New Zealand by 50 percent.

• • •

The history of SIDS is not as long as one may think; in fact, the term "Sudden Infant Death Syndrome" was not even developed until 1969. The most recent definition of SIDS reads: "SIDS is the sudden death of an infant under one year of age that remains unexplained after a thorough case investigation, including performance of a complete autopsy, examination of the death scene, and review of the clinical history." Why did it take so long for a definition to emerge for a syndrome that some say has its first recorded occurrence in the Bible story of King Solomon? (Not to mention the most famous example of safe sleep—a certain baby whose wise mother "wrapped him in swaddling clothes, and laid him in a manger.")

Many deaths that were regularly termed SIDS in the twentieth century were classified in earlier centuries (perhaps millennia) as suffocation or overlay—when adults roll over on babies who are sharing their beds.

Looking back to Ancient Greece, we learn that overlay by the mother was common enough to have its own punishment. (Mothers of overlaid infants were required to hold the deceased child for three days and spend a year eating only bread and water.) German records from 1291 show an official dictum forbidding mothers to share their beds with children three years old or younger. Likewise, England and Italy both had laws and penalties, dating to the fourteenth and sixteenth centuries, respectively, for overlaying an infant, with the Italians even accusing older women of witchcraft for the crime of killing babies and replacing them in the beds of their parents. Punishments in seventeenth-century Sweden included mothers being pilloried.

Scotland and England both recognized overlay as a common cause of death among infants, with the first three causes reported by the Scottish Surgeon of Police in 1892 being "1. ignorance and carelessness of mother 2. drunkenness 3. overcrowding." These were all in connection to overlay, leading to the passage of Scottish laws that year prohibiting parents from sleeping with their infants. Not only did the Scottish recognize overlay as a danger, but they also noted that "inattention to style, weight, and fit of infant clothing and the misuse of pillows, rubber sheets, easily untucked sheets, blankets and unnecessary decorative articles for cribs and carriages were potential causes of infant suffocation."

W. B. Yeats captured the anguish of a mother who had overlain her infant in the 1889 poem, "The Ballad of Moll Magee."

> *I lay upon my baby;*
> *Ye little childer dear,*
> *I looked on my cold baby*
> *When the morn grew frosty and clear.*
> *A weary woman sleeps so hard!*
> *My man grew red and pale,*
> *And gave me money, and bade me go*
> *To my own place, Kinsdale.*
> *…So now ye little childer*
> *You won't fling stones at me*
> *But gather with your shinin' looks*
> *and pity Moll Magee.*

An article in *The British Medical Journal* published on August 10, 1895, was written as a response to the large number of infant deaths in the winter months in England. The British medical community claimed these infants had been overlaid "or more probably suffocated under the bedclothes, during the sleep." Since it was felt that Parliament would not pass legislation forbidding mothers to sleep in the same beds as infants, the medical community looked to their Continental counterparts for advice on how to alleviate the problem. The *Cyclopedia of Obstetrics*, published in Manchester, England, in 1849 by Dr. Charles Clay, told of a device called an *arcuccio* that had been used since the sixteenth century by Italian mothers to prevent overlay. A Dr. Stuart Tidey made further inquiries for the *British Medical Journal* and found the arcuccio still in use in 1895. The device was placed in bed between the parents, the child was laid within it, and the bedclothes were pulled over the arcuccio with an uncovered space left at the top. This was so successful in preventing overlay and suffocation that from 1888 to 1895 in Tuscany, only one child was found to have died of overlay or suffocation. The use of the arcuccio was so common that nurses in Florence put themselves in danger of excommunication if they did not use them when putting children down to sleep. If a mother failed to use the arcuccio and her infant died, not only would she face charges for "homicide by negligence" (and perhaps censure by the church, according to some sources), but she would also be reviled in the community, "which would judge very severely any mother whose child lost its life owing to failure to use a well recognized precaution."

While overlay and suffocation were still seen as real dangers, other possible causes for infant deaths began to surface at the turn of the nineteenth century. As responsibility for the punishment of parents of overlaid infants shifted from the church to the state, the need for scientific evidence of cause of death became necessary, and the medical establishment for the first time began to study infant-death patterns as they fulfilled court requests for infant autopsies. As cribs and cradles became more common, it seemed less likely to people that these infant deaths were being caused by unsafe sleep practices. Although stomach sleeping, loose or overstuffed bedclothes, and overcrowding of the crib by toys or bumper pads can all present suffocation dangers, these new sleeping environments that were separated from the parents must have seemed the epitome of safety. Doctors and other authorities began looking for alternative theories to suffocation and overlay for unexplained infant death.

The Thymus Theory of SIDS became popular in the early part of the twentieth century when doctors noted the relatively large size of the thymus gland among infants they were autopsying. Because of the thymus's location—between the lungs and behind the sternum—doctors hypothesized that perhaps the thymus gland was interfering with breathing or with the rhythm of the heart and was a cause of sudden death among infants and children. Although the thymus theory was abandoned fairly quickly as a cause of infant sudden death, from 1926 to 1947 it was common practice for doctors to irradiate the thymus gland in children prior to elective surgical procedures such as tonsillectomy to decrease the risk of morbidity and even mortality following these procedures. (It wasn't until later that doctors learned that the thymus gland is always larger in children and that it plays an essential role in the immune system as the source of T lymphocytes and in controlling the metabolism of calcium in the body through the parathyroid glands, which are located within the gland. Since autopsying infants was a new practice and the science of understanding the role of the thymus gland was nonexistent, these facts were unknown. Also not established until later was that adults who underwent thymic radiation as children would have a risk of thyroid cancer that was 18.6 times as high as that of their unexposed siblings.) For the first time, there was a possible scientific explanation that absolved mothers of blame in the cause of unexplained infant death. Prosecutions and accusations of negligence waned. However, infant mortality rates did not.

In 1944, Dr. Harold Abramson of the New York City Committee on Infant Mortality published the results of a four-year study on infant deaths attributed to "accidental mechanical suffocation" and discovered that 68 percent of infants were found sleeping on their stomachs, with 50 percent having the nose or mouth in contact with bedding. From 1942 to 1953, Drs. Jacob Werne and Irene Garrow of the Queens County Medical Examiner's Office published a series of articles refuting Abramson's research, stating that attributing infant deaths to suffocation "increased the feeling of culpable negligence experienced by the mother." They shifted the focus back to medical causes of SIDS, claiming that fulminating infection was the likely cause, with emphasis on the respiratory system.

As doctors became more befuddled, parents became more hopeless. Not only were we getting farther away from the cause (and cure), but the only known risk factors—victims were typically males between two and four months of age, and most deaths occurred in the winter—were nonmodifiable.

In the 1960s, families of SIDS victims created the Guild for Infant Survival and the National SIDS Foundation with the intention of providing grief support and encouraging research. Partially in response to pressure from these groups, the National Institute of Child Health and Human Development (NICHD) sponsored two conferences on SIDS in an attempt to encourage doctors to engage in SIDS research. In the 1963 Conference Conclusion Statement, they reported that "the number of infants who die of the sudden death syndrome is of a comparable order of magnitude to the number of adults who die from carcinoma of the lung. Despite this fact the information is minuscule in comparison to that on carcinoma of the lung."

The 1969 NICHD conference was attended by an international audience that included researchers and parents who had lost babies to SIDS. At this pivotal event, the modern definition of SIDS was crafted, leaving behind the term "crib death," a misnomer that had led many people to believe the crib itself responsible. Parents at the conference were encouraged to lobby Congress to fund research and support for grieving parents. This pressure on the government, along with the claim of researchers in 1970 that SIDS deaths were being underreported by as much as 90 percent because of the absence of a nationwide reporting and classification system, led to the Sudden Infant Death Act of 1974, which placed the responsibility for research and support services on the NICHD and Maternal and Child Health Bureau. The act greatly increased available funding for research and caused Congress to conduct hearings on the syndrome. In 1979, the World Health Organization first recognized SIDS as a cause of death.

The apnea theory of SIDS surfaced in 1972, which led to a spike in parents using monitors in their babies' nurseries. However, no SIDS death was ever stopped by a monitor. One bright spot was the recognition of some modifiable risk factors—prenatal exposure to cigarette smoke and low birth weight. Throughout the 1980s, research on SIDS reached a new high. The New York Academy of Science Congress on SIDS in 1987 focused mainly on possible causes relating to cardiac and respiratory issues. It was thought that perhaps babies were suffering hypoxia—low oxygenation of the blood. Aside from the heart and lungs, it was speculated that an underdeveloped brain stem could also keep babies who were having breathing issues from rousing and removing themselves from danger.

In other parts of the globe, researchers were finding sleep positioning a more compelling argument. In 1972 in the Netherlands, the preferred sleep position for infants changed from supine (on the back) to prone (on the stomach) fairly abruptly, and SIDS rates changed right along with it. The baseline incidence of SIDS in the Netherlands was 0.46/1000 live births. By 1986, after the recommendation to change the sleep position of the infant from back to stomach, that number had shot up to 1.3/1000 live births. Similarly, in 1986, Australian researchers discovered that as prone sleeping decreased, so did their rates of SIDS. These statistics were compelling enough to lead to the research presented at the 1992 conference in Sydney. There, we learned that since doctors under the advice of Mitchell's team had begun recommending back and side sleeping to parents, the SIDS rates in those countries had dropped 50 percent. (Side sleeping eventually fell out of favor in 1996 when it was decided that the chances of babies rolling over onto their stomachs were too high.)

In the lifetimes of those of us in attendance at the 1992 international conference, SIDS had always been a mystery—striking healthy babies seemingly at random. No one could tell parents how to prevent it or even offer warning signs. It could strike at any time from birth to one year. Baby monitors weren't effective in stopping it. In fact, babies had died in their mothers' arms with no warning.

Now, in 1992, Mitchell and his team were offering a practical solution to help solve what had come to be regarded as a medical mystery. And we, a room full of professionals and parents who had devoted our lives to this cause, were elated but also flabbergasted. Could it really be as simple as sleep position? Thanks to Ed Mitchell and his team of researchers, we had hope. We might not know *why* babies were dying on their stomachs, but we had a preventative measure with strong data to recommend it.

I wondered how long it would take until we could see this change in the States, worried that perhaps lengthy research and intensive lobbying would be needed to convince doctors to impart this advice to parents. However, within three months, Dr. Marian Willinger of the National Institutes of Health was on *Good Morning America* imploring parents to place infants on their backs or sides to sleep. In 1994 the American Academy of Pediatrics (AAP) endorsed Back to Sleep. By 2000, US SIDS rates had dropped 50 percent.

Amazing, thrilling, fantastic, right? Of course. At the time of the 1992 international conference in

Australia, approximately ten thousand babies were dying of SIDS each year in the United States. The Back to Sleep campaign helped save the lives of over five thousand babies each year. However, when you deal in babies' lives, a number like that must be looked at as a glass-half-empty scenario. What about the other 50 percent? Why did the rate of SIDS plateau in the 1990s? Why were babies still dying? Was our education about placing babies on their backs to reduce the risk of SIDS not reaching all caregivers? In 1998 Eileen and I decided to look at the data in Allegheny County and noticed a different pattern—babies were being placed on their backs, but they were not in safe cribs. They were in adult beds, on couches, or in other unsafe sleep environments.

The simplicity of Back to Sleep encouraged us. Perhaps we could save all our babies through a similarly simple intervention.

Lesson 2

● ● ●

DON'T WAIT FOR SOMEONE ELSE
TO SOLVE YOUR PROBLEMS.

**Consider that you may be
the expert you seek.**

*There will come a time when you
believe that everything is finished.*

That will be the beginning.

—Louis L'Amour

During the humid Pittsburgh summer of 1998, four parents woke up to find their babies dead in bed next to them. Police Commander Gwen Elliott was livid. In her mind, these were preventable deaths—suffocation in sheets and blankets, adults rolling over on helpless infants—and she wondered if police action should be taken. Obviously, no one wants to compound the anguish of a grieving parent, but Elliot was thinking of the babies. Isn't it a basic moral responsibility to help those who can't help themselves?

She contacted Allegheny County District Attorney Stephen Zappala for his opinion. Since the parents hadn't broken any laws, he was wary. It didn't seem they could be charged with negligence either, having an infant sleep in bed with an adult wasn't universally considered an unsafe practice. Some parents did it; others didn't. What was the rule, anyway? As a young father, he had been taught to put his children on their backs to sleep, but no one had ever said much about *where* they should sleep. His gut told him that prevention was a better approach than punishment.

In the meantime, we at SIDS of Pennsylvania (our chapter had undergone a name change when we'd taken over SIDS services throughout the commonwealth) had found that while the Back to Sleep Campaign had been a godsend, in 1997 the rates had plateaued. Instead of eliminating all SIDS deaths, back sleeping had only stopped 50 percent of them. Eileen, who was completing her master of social work degree and working for us part-time, was still our main parent contact, facilitating our support meetings with assistance from Joe Fung, a SIDS father who has been with our organization through all its permutations since the 1985 death of his daughter, Amanda. They noticed that while SIDS had previously seemed to be equal opportunity, the population of parents to whom they were providing outreach was becoming less diverse.

As Back to Sleep spread, fewer middle- to upper-class white babies were dying of SIDS, while the number of lower-income African-American babies wasn't changing. A logical conclusion was that perhaps the Back to Sleep message wasn't reaching the African-American population. For years, Dr. Cyril Wecht (who served as the county coroner off and on for decades) had sent us referrals of all local infants who had died of SIDS in an effort to help us identify parents in need of bereavement-support services. Not knowing where else to start, I asked him to send us his death-scene investigation forms too. From these more detailed reports we would be able to tell if the babies who'd died were sleeping on their backs, since in the event of death, the blood pools to the lowest point of the body—information the coroner would have documented.

Dr. Wecht asked Joe Dominick, a member of the Child Death Review Team and his Chief Deputy Coroner (who presently is the Chairman of the Cribs for Kids board of directors) and Stephen Koehler, head of the Forensic Epidemiological Department at the Allegheny

County Coroner's Office, to meet with us to discuss these findings. Stephen had done his doctoral dissertation on SIDS and was eager to be a part of the project.

Throughout the years we'd had a variety of neighbors in the rooms across the hall from us: Ask-A-Nurse, a hotline the hospital had set up to answer callers' medical questions; Pittsburgh Voyager, an educational nonprofit; and the Chronic Fatigue Syndrome Foundation. However, we happened to be neighborless when we requested the death-scene investigation forms from Dr. Wecht, so we piled them up in an empty room on a small, circular table and began to wade through them anytime grant writing or fund-raising or parent outreach weren't pulling us in other directions. Eileen and I spent lunches in there, met up in the early evening before heading home, and pored over the documents first thing in the morning before the day got away from us. We weren't sure what we were searching for, but we figured if we looked long enough, something would pop. So we kept reading the reports and talking about them as we did. *What area is that family from? Who found the baby? What time of day was it? This baby wasn't even in a crib. Was she on her back? Was he on his back? This baby wasn't even in a crib. This baby was on a couch. This baby was in bed with her mom. This baby wasn't in a crib. This baby was found on a beanbag chair! This baby wasn't in a crib. This baby was taking a nap on the recliner. Was she on her back? Was he on his back?*

It didn't take long to see the pattern. How many times had we said, "This baby wasn't in a crib"? How many times had we been stumped by the question, "Was the baby laid down on his back?" Who could say? A baby placed on his back to sleep on a couch or a chair could easily roll down a slanted cushion, land on his belly, and suffocate. On her back or not, an infant covered in heavy blankets or a parent's slumbering body is in for trouble. The vast majority of these babies—as many as 90 percent, we would eventually find out—hadn't been found in cribs. Rather, they had been laid down in adult beds, couches, recliners, and beanbag chairs. We'd started this search asking if the Back to Sleep message wasn't reaching low-income mothers, but we'd stumbled onto something we weren't expecting. What difference does sleep position make when a baby's sleep environment is fundamentally unsafe? We didn't want to jump the gun, but Eileen and I both felt like we were onto something big. If nothing else, our next step had presented itself to us. We needed to get these babies into cribs so that we could see if the SIDS rates would drop.

Right as we were making these connections and brainstorming the solutions, DA Zappala, who knew of my work through our board member City Councilman Bob O'Connor, called me to discuss this recent rash of deaths in the county. I shared our findings with him—not only had the four babies who'd died that summer not been in cribs, neither had most of the babies who'd died in our area in the past three years. He agreed with us that if babies were dying for the simple and tragic reason that their parents couldn't afford cribs, we had to do something about it. We began to discuss the possibility of providing cribs. The more we talked about it, the more it started to sound like a feasible idea. I recognized that education would be paramount to our success. If a mother didn't understand why putting her baby in a crib was important, having one in the house wasn't going to stop her from laying that baby down on a couch for a nap or bringing him into her bed to cuddle.

For the rest of the week, I worked on a proposal we could shop around to foundations to get seed money.

• • •

I was settling in in front of the TV with Dick the next Friday evening when the six o'clock news rolled footage of a press conference that the DA and Commander Elliot had called. They were asking people to bring their used cribs to Monroeville Mall the next day and imploring mothers without cribs to call the DA's office to receive one. Dick had been hearing impassioned work stories from me for long enough to know his quiet evening was over. "What is he doing? Used cribs? Is that even safe? What about the liability? We haven't even planned this out yet!" I typically wasn't one to spend all my time planning when there was work to be done—I'm all about digging in and getting my hands dirty—but this seemed premature even to me.

First thing Monday morning I called him. After the social niceties, I dove in.

"So how did your crib donation event work out?" I asked.

"It was a disaster!" he answered. I was relieved that he was inclined toward candor.

"Why? Didn't anyone show up?"

"Oh, plenty of people showed up. The problem was the cribs! I didn't realize how much wear and tear they go through. There were pieces missing, broken. Some of these things had to have been twenty years old. I don't know. I mean, people are really kind. They did what I asked them to do. They brought cribs, but we couldn't use any of them. In fact, the County had to dispose of them."

"That's a shame. Well, you gave it a shot, right?" I was thrilled that I wasn't charged with the indelicate job of explaining to the DA the liability issues of handing out used cribs. He was the legal mind, after all; I was just the chronic viewer of *Law and Order*.

"Oh, it's not over. I also asked mothers who needed cribs to put in requests with my office!"

"Oh, my." Pause. "So what did you tell them?" I asked with false innocence.

"Well, we took their names and told them we'd contact them this week. I mean, now that I know they don't have cribs, I'm responsible to help, right?"

"Well, it does seem that way."

"Where do I even start? This isn't exactly my wheelhouse. Seventy-two cribs! How am I going to get my hands on seventy-two cribs and distribute them to mothers who probably don't have cars?"

"Seventy-two? Hmmm."

"So…"

"Well, I suppose I could help," I offered nonchalantly, as if I hadn't been rehearsing this phone call all weekend.

"That would be great! What do we do?" Ah, the question I'd been waiting for.

"Well, off the top of my head, I'm thinking…OK, we have a new credit card with a ten-thousand-dollar limit. That should buy one hundred cribs. Luckily, we only need seventy-two. Let me call Toys "R" Us and see if they can help us. Maybe we can set up a voucher program with them? If we find a store on the bus line, moms won't have a problem with transportation, I guess. Can you take a crib on a bus?"

"Yes, we'll make it work! That sounds perfect!" Later Steve would tell me that he felt like the cavalry had shown up.

"Well, it's not that easy. I'm going to need to be reimbursed. This isn't exactly in our budget right now. Can you find a way to help me raise the money? Maybe there's a county budget that covers this kind of expense." Steve was new to his office and came from a prominent family. I knew he'd find a way to pay for the cribs. He'd better, or I was going to have some explaining to do to my board.

Our first stroke of luck came when we learned Toys "R" Us had cribs with mattresses on sale for $109. Our second stroke of luck was when the store manager was amenable to partnering with us and distributing the cribs from his location. Maybe it wasn't luck, actually—more of a logical reaction to hearing that he had an opportunity to help the DA out of a bind. Not a bad position to be in, surely.

We would need to be able to prove to donors that the mothers we were helping were truly in need, or they would be wary of helping us. We decided to require each mother to write us a letter stating that she had no safe place for her baby to sleep and include a copy of the baby's footprints. To our surprise, all seventy-two mothers obliged with beautiful letters pouring out their hearts, talking about how afraid they were that their babies might die sleeping on couches or in their beds. Next we worked with Toys "R" Us to create a tracking system so that people would not be able to return the cribs we gave away. We didn't want to have to worry about anyone in a pinch deciding they needed the money more than the crib.

Once we'd resolved those logistics, we were back to worrying about paying for this venture. That Friday I went to my monthly meeting of the South Side Rotary Club planning to ask for assistance. They were always looking for projects, ways to help the community. After all, that's what Rotary is all about. So I spoke up and asked for what I needed. I explained the crib project and how I was seeking donations to cover our costs. In addition to promises of spreading the word, I was given the mailing list of all fifty-one Rotary clubs in the county and the suggestion of writing a letter explaining the program and asking if each club could buy one crib.

I wasn't sure if our plight would resonate with the mostly older, male members of Rotary. They proved my skepticism wrong, however (as people and their goodness have done so many times over the years). Right away the money started rolling in. The response we received from the Braddock Rotary Club touched me most. Braddock, an eastern suburb of Pittsburgh, is a town that has struggled greatly since the collapse of the steel industry, having lost 90 percent of its population since the 1920s. This club that I know struggled financially in an area with so little viable business sent us a check for three cribs with a note that said, "We know that many of these cribs will come into our community. Thank you for looking out for our babies." I still choke up when I think of it, because I knew at that moment, "They get it!" Maybe we were onto something.

The next month at Rotary, I reported back about the strong response we'd already received. One of the Rotarians in my club was John Brown, who'd been a Steeler in the late sixties. It's hard to believe how differently NFL players were compensated in those days. After retiring from the game, many went into business, not just as a way to stay occupied but to make a living like the rest of us. Even though in some ways he was now my peer, he had been a hero to me when I watched him play. He would prove to be my hero again when he said, "If you can write me a proposal by next Wednesday, I'll take it to Ronald McDonald House Charities where I'm on the board. I think I can get you five thousand dollars."

I knew this was an opportunity to seize and went right back to my office to start writing. By the end of the week, I was dropping off the proposal at his office. Within a week from that day, he called to tell me that we'd gotten the money.

I called Steve and said, "You're not going to believe it. I think I'm going to be able to pay off the credit card soon. I got money from Ronald McDonald House and Rotary..."

He also had good news.

"That's great! *You're* not going to believe what *I* just discovered," he answered. "I've been poking around like you asked me to, looking for some budgets set aside for public safety, injury prevention, et cetera. DA Colville [his predecessor] set up this account for asset-forfeiture money. Anytime there's a drug bust or property is confiscated, the money from the auction goes into this account that is set aside 'to deter criminal activity.' We first started having this conversation because Gwen Elliott felt it was criminally negligent for a parent to roll over on her baby during sleep. And, well, I think if a baby dies because he doesn't have a crib, it's criminal. What do you think?" Of course, I agreed.

The asset-forfeiture money helped Steve match our Ronald McDonald House grant. We had our $10,000.

We worked quickly to get the cribs to the mothers, believing that each day we waited was a day their babies were in danger. We printed out crib vouchers from our office laser printer on SIDS of PA letterhead and put them in the mail. While it wasn't necessarily simple to maneuver crib boxes home on city buses, the mothers were pleased enough with our assistance that they made it work. The store manager carefully tracked the cribs and sent the vouchers back to us once they were collected. Within about a month, they had all been distributed, and I was asked to attend a check presentation at the Ronald McDonald House offices.

I invited Steve and Bob O'Connor to go with me. Steve was so excited by the success of the program that he decided to call some press contacts to attend. (It was a great opportunity for him to get positive publicity for the city and himself—the new, young DA—about whom people were still forming opinions. I didn't mind; clearly he deserved the praise.) What a surprise to me when all the local TV stations showed up! It didn't happen that way when *I* called a press conference. Ronald McDonald House Charities and Steve presented their checks, and we told the story of how we came to provide seventy-two cribs to at-risk families in hope of reducing the number of infant deaths throughout the county.

Everyone was aglow, even after the hot lights from the TV cameras were turned away from us. We headed home for the weekend with a feeling of accomplishment, patting ourselves on our backs for a job well done. What we hadn't realized yet was that this was a job that could never be finished.

I arrived at work on Monday morning with the phones ringing off the hook and a list of messages from the answering service as long as my arm. They all said the same thing: "I need a crib for my baby!"

Within two weeks, we had one hundred new requests. We knew then that this wasn't just a one-time event. It was too early to know if it was that next step to Back to Sleep, but we knew there was no moral way to say no to any of these mothers. Our new mission had begun.

Part of what strikes people when they hear the Cribs for Kids story is that it doesn't involve years of scientific research and experiments. Most people assume that the concept of safe-sleep environments must have come out of a medical school and been introduced to the world via a professional journal. It seems more likely than two women with no medical expertise whatsoever finding a commonality among thousands of infant deaths, while a police chief and a district attorney a few miles away are grappling over the same issue. I admit, it's uncanny, a perfect example of what we've come to call "the hand of God". My relationship with Eileen has always seemed destined, though. A few months after I started working for SIDS, she mentioned casually that her maiden name was Tasillo. In a flash, memories of her as a little girl in pigtails with big brown eyes washed over me. A lifetime earlier, my aunt Alvera and uncle Buddy Keene had been best friends with her parents. She and I were two of a whole gaggle of kids—babies through teens—who spent evenings at

Aunt Alvera's house when the grown-ups got together to play cards and drink Iron City beer. Our friendship was cemented in that moment of realization. Knowing that we shared that common experience, came up in the same corner of the world, and had been brought together again through this cause, bonded us.

Over the years we have had many successes but have endured heartbreak too, especially early on when there was so little that we understood about SIDS. For as long as I can remember, Eileen has had a quote taped to her computer monitor that says, "The purpose of life is not to be happy. It is to be useful, to be honorable, to be compassionate, to have it make some difference that you have lived and lived well." During those moments when I wonder how she finds the strength to face some of the tasks of our work—counseling grieving parents, watching the grim presentations at the Child Death Review meetings we attend each month—I think of that quote, and I realize that's the key to it all for her. Much like the old yarn about the misguided man who prays to God every day to win the lottery but never buys a ticket, we have learned that you can't stand around with your hands in your pockets if you want God's hand to reach out to you. Along with believing in yourself and your path, you have to take action.

Everyone in this chapter identified a problem and set out to solve it. Eileen and I had a problem: babies in

Allegheny County were still dying in spite of the Back to Sleep message. We could have just continued to do our jobs—raising money and awareness, counseling grieving parents—until a researcher or someone at our national organization made the discovery that many babies were sleeping in unsafe environments. Instead, we pulled together our resources and searched for an answer ourselves. Commander Elliott had a problem: her city was losing babies to preventable deaths. She could have turned her head, figuring these deaths were in a gray area that was probably outside her wheelhouse. Instead she spoke to the district attorney and asked the question, "Is this accident or negligence?" After careful thought, Steve's answer was *accident*. That could easily have ended his involvement, but instead he took action. That action was the link that brought our paths together.

As you walk your path, you may stumble on a problem that you feel compelled to solve. Listen to this compulsion. It just might be the hand of God (or spirit, universe, fate, positive thinking, whichever enlightened force you believe in) giving you a push. Don't make the mistake of excusing yourself because you think you're not the right person for the job. It's true that you might not have the necessary expertise, but maybe the expert needs you to ask the right question. Consider it your duty to at least seek out that expert and offer your services. Your contribution might be bringing the problem to the surface, connecting the right people, or perhaps taking a more active role. Whatever your part is, play it.

Don't discount the idea that *you* are the expert or could become the expert. It was shocking to me when we stumbled upon the knowledge that most babies in our county were dying while sleeping somewhere other than a crib. Should it have been a surprise to me, though, that Eileen and I would be the ones to make that discovery? Between us we had over twenty-five years of experience in dealing with unexpected infant deaths. We'd been studying SIDS research for years, had heard hundreds of people's personal stories about SIDS, knew our county's infant-death statistics inside and out, knew the populations who were and were not being affected, and had a strong relationship with our coroner's office, who gave us access to death-scene investigation reports.

What it came down to was our belief that we could do it. If we hadn't believed in our own power, we would have never even tried. "We'll leave that to the experts," we'd figure. Who were the experts? We were.

Lesson 3

● ● ●

DON'T LET YOUR JOB GET IN THE WAY OF YOUR WORK.

A ship in harbor is safe, but that's not what ships are built for.

—John A. Shedd

For the next few years, we were like apostles of a new religion, barefoot and in rags, spreading the good word about safe sleep far and wide and putting all the money we scraped together right back into the cause. For most nonprofits, increased awareness means increased donations; for us it meant more money being spent as we tried to fulfill every crib request. Even with the addition of new fund raisers like Kayla's Run for SIDS, the Cribs for Kids Golf Tournament, and our annual parties where we raffled off a walk-on role on the television show *Scrubs*—compliments of board member Noreen Crowell's son, Sean, who was a key grip on the long-running comedy—we struggled to keep money in the bank. Saying no to a mother in need, or even putting her off for a few months, meant a baby was in danger. No wasn't an option.

Finding grants that met our needs was an additional challenge. Foundations typically fund research or provide money to hire employees, not buy tangible items. Giving us money to buy cribs didn't fit into most funders' missions. Those who were willing to consider us questioned our anecdotal research. While Eileen and I may have accepted our role as experts, others weren't so easily swayed. They wanted to see articles in peer-reviewed journals telling of thousands of hours of study by medical professionals. Who had time for that? The research was all around us every day as we continued to educate mothers, provide cribs and watch the SIDS rates fall in the areas we were servicing. How many more babies would die during the years it would take to complete research and publish results? "But who gave you the authority to do this?" was a common question. As far as I was concerned, there was no possible danger in what we were doing, so no one had to give us permission. All babies deserve their own places to sleep, and that's what we were providing. It was a hard sell to donors, though. Not many people want to give away large sums of money to someone who says, "Trust me."

The SIDS community got it. Our phones were lighting up with calls from infant advocates around Pennsylvania who wanted to know what we had done to reduce our SIDS rates by over 60 percent in Allegheny County since the late '90s. We realized we had to find opportunities to tell our story to doubters, walk them through our thought processes so they could see how we had connected the dots. While we didn't feel we could invest the time or money in a years-long study, we couldn't deny that having statistics to back us up would be helpful. Eileen asked her teacher at University of Pittsburgh, Dr. Helen Petracchi, to sponsor her to do a directed study of the progress of Cribs for Kids. Dr. Petracchi agreed and connected her to another assistant professor at the School of Social Work, Dr. Kathryn S. Collins. Together, they designed a study that would ascertain how the program was working—for example, if the mothers who received the cribs were using them, and where their infants would have slept if not for the donated cribs. They created a qualitative/quantitative questionnaire containing eighteen questions related to each SIDS risk reduction point outlined by the Back to Sleep Campaign. The questionnaire was administered by phone and took approximately ten to fifteen minutes to complete. Of the 150 attempts, 105 were completed, a response rate of 70 percent.

The results were encouraging. Most notably, every participant reported that she used the crib as a safe sleeping environment for her infant; two-thirds reported placing their infants in the supine position. When queried where their infants would have slept if they had not received cribs from Cribs for Kids, over one-third (38 percent) reported that their infants would have slept in adult beds with the parents, one-quarter in bassinets, and the remainder on the floor or in portable cribs. A majority (seventy-five) of the participants with other children reported that when those children were infants, they had slept in old cribs that were in poor condition.

Eileen and I took our story and data to our local health department, coroner, hospitals, and social-services groups. Once we had their endorsements, we extended our reach throughout the state, setting up meetings and attending conferences with groups like Safe Kids USA and Pennsylvania Child Death Review (PA CDR). We involved the medical community by lecturing at grand rounds at various hospitals.

I had been a member of the Allegheny County Child Death Review Team since its inception in 1997. When I received an invitation to the annual statewide CDR conference in Harrisburg, I saw it as the perfect networking venue. The PA CDR was created as part of a national organization to investigate all deaths of children from birth to twenty-one in the hope of preventing child deaths whenever possible. What better venue for sharing our mission? Through my experience on our local team, I had found that CDR teams throughout the commonwealth were weary of investigating deaths of babies dying suddenly and unexpectedly, in spite of the fact that SIDS is the leading cause of death from birth to age one. People were jaded to SIDS. *Why investigate? We know what it is, and we know we can't change it* seemed to be the prevailing attitude. Sharing our story with this group could make a real impact. If they knew that there was data that they could collect at these death scenes that could help us to learn more about unsafe sleep and prevent infant deaths, their attitudes might shift.

I called to RSVP and was greeted by the friendly, warm voice of Vick Zittle, the program director of PA CDR. After introductions, I gave her a brief synopsis of our work and the decrease in SIDS rates in Allegheny County. That was all it took to make her a Cribs for Kids advocate. To my delight, she insisted that I not only attend the conference but also accept her donation of an exhibit table where we could showcase our work. The conference was scheduled for late September 2002, giving me only two weeks to prepare.

When I arrived at the conference, I realized there was an additional reason to be glad I'd made the trip. Charlie LaVallee, executive director of Highmark's Caring Place, was in attendance and invited me personally to attend his session so that he could acknowledge me as one of the cocreators (with Bob O'Connor) of the Pittsburgh Center for Grieving Children, which had become the Caring Place. I was hurrying out of Charlie's session and back to my exhibit table when I quite literally bumped into Dr. Eileen Tyrala. (This is a moment I consider personally and professionally historic, as she would become a great friend and medical director of Cribs for Kids.) After our collision, we apologized and introduced ourselves. When she asked me for more information about our program, I took her to my table and gave her the full presentation. Eileen is a pediatrician and neonatologist from Philadelphia and a member of the PA AAP CDR team, as well as a Fellow in the American Academy of Pediatrics— definitely someone I wanted to convert. It ended up she was an easy sell. "We have to do this in Philly!" she told me right away. "I'm tired of having to tell parents that I don't know why they lost their child. It's too heart wrenching. If this program can prevent those deaths, count me in one hundred percent."

Eileen started helping us promote Cribs for Kids in Philadelphia. She had lived and worked there all her life and was passionate about driving down their SIDS rates. In November she called to tell me that she'd set up a meeting with Maternity Care Coalition (MCC). We'd been trying to build a relationship with the Philadelphia Department of Public Health for years to no avail, so we jumped at this entrée to their community. In January, I drove east and presented at MCC's board meeting, signing them on as a partner.

As we expanded our services, we realized that our system of buying full-sized cribs and mattresses from Toys "R" Us was serviceable but not ideal. Transporting unwieldy crib boxes home on buses continued to be a difficulty, and cribs were often left behind when families moved, which was a common occurrence for our transient clients. We often received phone calls from mothers struggling to assemble the cribs. (I got a new appreciation for this when my grandson, Jack, was born, and Dick and I spent a harried evening preparing our guest room for his visits.) We were at a loss as to how to instruct them. Bob O'Connor and Steve Zappala came up with the clever idea of enlisting the University of Pittsburgh chapter of Delta Tau Delta to be our crib crew. When we received a call from a mother who needed a hand, we'd contact the fraternity house and round up a group of guys to make a house call. Just as often, though, mothers would rely on their social-services agencies for help with this task. We weren't very popular with our local public-health nurses when they had to start carrying toolboxes on their home visits.

As we were grappling with this problem, we got several crib requests that we couldn't fill. We had enough money to buy fifty, but we needed one hundred. Our choices were leaving fifty babies without cribs or finding a cheaper alternative. We went on a fact-finding mission to the Toys "R" Us store in Monroeville, Pennsylvania, about thirty minutes from our offices, and found the Graco Pack 'n Play. The Pack 'n Play is a "playard" that functions as a bassinet for babies up to fifteen pounds and then easily converts into a crib for babies up to thirty pounds. At $69.99 they were our cheapest option. Worried that our mothers would be dissatisfied, we said, "Just this one time, we're going to buy these playards, just to get us out of this jam."

We were thrilled when we started getting thank-you notes from mothers full of praise for the Graco Pack 'n Play. Not only were these units easy to assemble; they were portable. This made it easier to schlep them home from the store, and for the first time, our moms were able to take their cribs anywhere they took their babies. Infants weren't just sleeping safely at home but at Grandma's, Auntie's, and the babysitter's. The playards solved our issue of portability and were 30 percent cheaper than full-sized cribs. We'd solved two problems with one solution while managing to make babies safer.

Jackpot! This system began to work so well for us that as we fielded calls from people who were interested in our program, we encouraged them to set up the same system with their local Toys "R" Us stores.

In November of that year, Michaelleene, Eileen, and I headed to Orlando for the annual SIDS Alliance national conference. We had brought Eileen on full-time, through a grant from Heinz Endowments, as our director of support and education when she finished her MSW. (Her first day as a full-time employee was August 12, 2002, which would have been Rachel's twenty-second birthday. "I felt like she was giving me her blessing," she says.)

The holidays and our Christmas Gift Wrap approaching made this a busy time, but the conference was a permanent fixture on our calendar in those days. It was an invaluable chance to share with our colleagues around the country our challenges and successes in fund-raising, grant writing, and lobbying, as well as learn more about the latest research developments directly from the doctors who were engaged in that work. I had written a proposal to speak about Cribs for Kids and was disappointed it hadn't been accepted, but I figured there would be plenty of informal opportunities to spread the word. After years of networking my way through these events, I'd made many strong alliances and friendships in the SIDS community. If history were any indicator, I'd be spending my evenings with them catching up over long dinners and drinks.

We arrived at the hotel midafternoon, checked in at the front desk, and dropped our luggage in the room. Money was tight, and with airfare, meals, and registration costs, it would be an expensive week. Sharing a hotel room was one area where we could economize.

Once we were settled, we headed to registration. Although we had taken the elevator to the floor the concierge had directed us to, something didn't seem right. All the banners and posters decorating the common areas were for an organization called First Candle. (We had never heard of First Candle but assumed it must have something to do with raising money for 9/11 victims, since the ascenders on the "d" and "l" in the word *candle* had a flame above them, making them look like the Twin Towers.) Familiar faces and friendly waves from behind a long table covered in clipboards and nametags assured us that we had reached our destination, though. "Don't miss the Welcome Reception tonight. There's a big announcement," we were told as we loaded ourselves down with armfuls of presentation materials and agendas. We assured them, of course, that we would never miss an event that included wine, cheese, and old friends.

In spite of its name, the Welcome Reception felt anything but. Tom Harris, a board member of SIDS Alliance (National, as we referred to it), began his talk that night simply and positively with a report of the wonderful progress in reducing SIDS deaths that had been made over the past six or seven years. In fact, the Back to Sleep Campaign had been so successful, he informed us, that SIDS Alliance had decided to expand their focus from SIDS to include deaths caused by stillbirth and miscarriage. The organization's new name would be First Candle, to reflect "the commitment we have to helping all babies reach that important milestone, their first birthday, but also the hope and the light that we help to provide to bereaved parents," the first press release said.

For a moment you could hear a pin drop; then all hell broke loose.

To outsiders it may not be obvious why this announcement was met with outrage. After all, inclusiveness is usually considered a virtue. None of us were insensitive to the pain of mothers who lose children through stillbirth or miscarriage; I had had three miscarriages myself and knew that anguish personally. Our concern was that SIDS Alliance was leaving their work unfinished, losing focus on the cause just as we were beginning to make progress. What had happened to the dream of eliminating SIDS? A 50 percent decrease in rates was gratifying progress, not victory. We felt like we were being handed the trophy and sent home at half-time. Adding insult to injury, the affiliates who had kept the organization financially afloat hadn't had any input in this major decision. Now we found ourselves standing dumbly, mouths full of cheese and crackers, while our new mission statement was rolled out to us.

I think National was aware that this was not going to be an easy conversation. I assume that's why they dropped the bomb that first night, to give attendees a chance to digest and accept the changes before the formal sessions began the next morning. However, they underestimated just how disorienting and devastating this news would be for so many. A great number of the conference attendees were parents who had devoted their lives to the cause after losing their children. To them, this announcement felt like the world was giving up on the still-mysterious killer that had taken their babies. SIDS Alliance had been the leader in the SIDS movement since 1991 when they'd called together the other major SIDS groups in the United States and convinced them that one organization would be more successful in fighting for our cause than multiple groups. And now, ten years later, they were de-emphasizing SIDS to the point of changing their name.

The SIDS Alliance board maintained that remaining an organization focused solely on SIDS was becoming unsustainable for a number of reasons. According to a missive they wrote entitled "A Letter to Our Constituency," there was a "public perception that the mystery of SIDS had been solved" because of the drop in SIDS rates. As a result, funding from traditional sources was drying up. Corporations, foundations, and private donors no longer saw SIDS as a significant enough child-health issue to garner their attention. Furthermore, the number of scientists studying SIDS was dwindling. In order to remain viable, they felt their only choice was to expand their mission.

It seemed ironic that the success the SIDS community had been seeking for decades was leading to our dissolution. Perhaps that's the deal you make when you work for a nonprofit. You toil in the hope that someday you will eliminate a problem or issue, eventually making yourself obsolete. If only that were the case.

Naturally, the conference schedule was jam-packed with speakers, trainings, and information sessions on any number of topics, but there was only one thing on our minds. Every gathering that week turned into a discussion about the changed mission as we rehashed the announcement and tried to adjust to this new worldview. The night after the Welcome Reception, there were about ten people gathered in my hotel room venting, trying to get our minds around the events of the past twenty-four hours. We were interrupted by a knock on the door. Gerri Alfano, a SIDS mother who worked for one of the New York affiliates, was standing there vibrating with energy, her springy, black hair standing on end. She walked in and began talking heatedly in her thick Long Island accent. She had just been in an education session that had quickly devolved into a shouting match.

"I just can't believe this is happening," she said. "They started going through this same BS from last night again, all of their reasons why. Finally this woman stood up and started screaming, 'This isn't right. You can't do this. How can you change the focus of our organization? We've been funding you forever!' She was going out of her mind, really letting them have it. All of a sudden, I looked down and realized that woman was me!" Apparently in her disbelief and rage, she'd had an out-of-body experience. Gerri gave us one of our only laughs of the week with that story, but for all of us, including her, a SIDS mother who'd been supporting SIDS Alliance for years, this was no laughing matter.

As the week wore on, the content of our conversations changed. Many of us felt there was still a great deal of work to be done to eliminate SIDS, yet we feared support from National would be minimal. "The bottom line is our name is changed, our mission is changed, so get over it," seemed to be their final word. But we couldn't, and, more importantly, we felt we shouldn't. So instead of trying to adjust, we began to consider moving forward without First Candle. The thought of striking out on our own was daunting, but not as daunting as the seismic shift in mind-set that would be required to stay. What did leaving mean? Would we exist as independent organizations? If so, could we thrive without a national organization to guide us? Perhaps we should create a new national organization. What did that entail, and how long would it take? I wondered if this would help the Cribs for Kids campaign to grow or take my attention from it. There were so many questions and no clear answers.

Later that week, I was approached by a senior member of First Candle staff. To my surprise I was asked to serve on their national board. Never before had they offered me an opportunity at such a high level. I wondered if I had misjudged their intentions. Our work at SIDS of PA had been increasingly focused on the Cribs for Kids campaign for the past four years. Perhaps this offer was a sign that they'd finally seen its value. With input at the national level, I could help ensure that SIDS research and prevention still received proper support and use that platform to expand Cribs for Kids throughout the country.

"There are still thousands of babies dying each year. I believe Cribs for Kids is the next step to Back to Sleep, and that's where I would want to focus," I began.

"Judy, don't you understand? That's not where we're heading. If we take on stillbirth, we'll have thirty thousand feet on the street raising money for us!"

That statement caught me off guard. It seemed like money was being placed above mission. When did we start confusing *our jobs* with *our work*?

All the uncertainty of the week, all the wondering what direction to take, had brought me to a fork in the road. Thankfully, this conversation in the twilight had turned on the streetlights. At once I could read the signs. It was time to choose—this job or my work. National had never really embraced Cribs for Kids before, and they weren't looking to start now. My success as a fund raiser was why they had offered me a place on the board. In fact, it was what had always gotten me their praise and attention. I was proud of our successes in development; that money fueled everything we did. But it was the means to the end, not the end itself. If I took this position on the national board and SIDS of PA remained part of First Candle, we'd have a guide to follow, but we'd be heading down the wrong path. I'd had many jobs throughout my life, but it wasn't until I answered that phone call from Ray Mansfield in 1989 that I found my work, my true north. It was time to let go of the familiar and the safe and let that magnetic pull carry me onward.

My flight back to Pittsburgh only lasted a few hours, but I traveled home with the suspicion that I had set off on a new leg of my life's journey.

Lesson 4

●   ●   ●

DON'T GET HUNG UP ON THE
HOWS OF YOUR DREAMS.

**If you see your dreams clearly, the
hows take care of themselves.**

*Life is what happens to you while
you're busy making other plans.*

—John Lennon

Every few years a news story surfaces about physicists finding evidence supporting the theory that multiple universes exist in parallel to ours, places where actions and decisions in opposition to our own have created different paths of existence. I don't know anything about quantum physics, but I am reasonably sure that a universe without First Candle is a universe where Cribs for Kids remained a local concern, an offshoot of SIDS of PA. When SIDS Alliance changed its name and mission, we were pushed to redefine ourselves, too. Being one of many affiliates of a national organization had kept us thinking locally, focused on our rates in Pennsylvania instead of nationally or worldwide. Those regional boundaries disappeared when we considered separating from First Candle. The nagging fear that National wasn't interested in Cribs for Kids, that they didn't want to put it on their agenda, began to fall away. Concerns like not being asked to speak at the conference or waiting and hoping for someone else to promote our program to the other affiliates receded into the background. For the first time, we were looking out at a limitless horizon. Cribs for Kids had its own mission, and now we'd gained permission to chart our own course.

Sometimes we aren't ready to accept freedom when it presents itself, though. While I believed in our program wholeheartedly, I had no idea how I would take it beyond Allegheny County. We were struggling to provide cribs to mothers in our community; where would I find the money to create and run a national organization? So I kept my dreams of expansion to myself and spent more time listening than speaking—which is unlike me, frankly—when talk turned to next steps. I got on board with the idea of helping create a new national SIDS organization of which Cribs for Kids could be a part. Sometimes I fantasized that someone else, preferably someone with deep pockets, would float the idea that Cribs for Kids should *be* that organization. But then my cautious side—the least successful side of me—would speak up and bring me down to earth.

Looking back, I can see that I went against all my instincts. I was trying to deny my dream and was following when I wanted to lead. Both of those actions are in contrast to my essential nature. Every time I have found success, it has been through thinking big and taking action, yet there I was letting myself be so intimidated by the hows—*How would we find the money? How would we structure the organization? How would we distribute cribs throughout the country?*—that I tried to convince myself that I was dreaming the wrong dream.

• • •

I sometimes wonder if SIDS of PA would have remained part of First Candle longer if the name and mission change had been announced via conference call or in a written communication. When it was announced at the conference, reactions were obvious and immediate. Had we received the news privately in our offices, there might have been a period of tactful phone calls and ambiguous e-mails feeling out colleagues around the SIDS community. Instead, all we had to do was look around to see whose jaw was dropping, whose nostrils were flared. What's more, we had days together to chew it over. Like homesick campers, we could talk and talk about all levels of our discomfiture from breakfast to campfire chat (which in our case took place around the hotel bar).

This was when I really got to know Judy Rainey, who is now Cribs for Kids' director of national and legislative affairs. In 1996 her son Joe was at his day-care across the street from her office, sitting in his high chair eating lunch, when he suddenly collapsed and died. He was eight months old. Since his death was unexplained, the medical examiner called it SIDS. Judy became involved with a local SIDS group where she attended support meetings and eventually became president of the Northern Virginia SIDS Alliance.

Judy grew up in Virginia in a family heavily involved in the military and in government. Her father, Stan Kimmitt, was a retired army colonel who served as secretary of the Senate and was the founder of a lobbying firm. Summers during college, Judy had internships in the Senate, and after graduation she took a job with the Senate sergeant at arms when she couldn't find a teaching position. She expected to stay at the

Senate no more than two years; thirty-two years later, she retired after working in administrative positions for a variety of senators, including Jay Rockefeller of West Virginia, Bob Kerrey of Nebraska, Tom Carper of Delaware, and Frank Lautenberg of New Jersey.

Judy's the type of person who gets things done. She's happiest when she's identifying a problem and working to solve it. In 1982 when she was struggling with child-care for her children, she worked with a group of Senate colleagues to open the Senate Employees Child Care Center. In 1992 she designed a computerized personnel program for Senate offices and committees that is still used today. Judy's passion is sharing best practices. She led the Democratic Administrative Managers Group for ten years and created the first bipartisan Administrative Steering Committee, which works with groups through-out the Senate to improve the effectiveness and efficiency of running Senate offices. Following in her father's and brother's footsteps, she is also a longtime board member of the US Senate Federal Credit Union.

The first time I saw her name was on a flyer about a listserv she had started for the SIDS community. I didn't even know what a listserv was, and she was starting one! Because I kept this gold piece of paper, with all the login information and the explanation of how and when to use the listserv, hanging on the filing cabinet next to my desk for years, I saw her name every day. At the First

Candle conference, she was one of the most vocal people speaking out against the mission and name change. We struck up a conversation there one day, and I felt like I was meeting a minor celebrity. She told me she had been following Cribs for Kids' progress since she'd first heard me speak at a conference in 1999. It didn't take long to realize we were kindred spirits.

When the conference ended, there were more questions than answers. Judy set up another e-mail listserv and invited those of us who were still unsure how to move forward to share our ideas, visions, frustrations, and questions. The idea of leaving First Candle to form a new national organization began to gain traction. Of course, that was a step not to be taken lightly. It would be time-consuming and expensive, perhaps pulling our focuses from our missions for years while we set up the new entity. To give us a chance to explore this option deeper, I offered to host a meeting in Pittsburgh after the holidays for anyone who was interested.

SIDS of PA had little money to spare, but I scraped together enough to hire a facilitator and, along with some of the other guests, chipped in for airfare and hotel rooms for those who needed the extra help. Having a facilitator was crucial. We all had an emotional stake in this work and needed someone unbiased who could steer us in the direction that made the most sense from a professional standpoint. Other than that, the weekend was no-frills. People flew in Friday evening, we met all day Saturday, and they left Sunday morning.

• • •

On a Friday evening in February 2003, thirteen representatives from ten SIDS organizations spanning from New York to Washington State arrived at the airport Hyatt outside of Pittsburgh to begin distilling ideas into actions. The attendees were mostly from the larger affiliates, the greatest financial contributors to the national organization. Affiliates were required to pay 10 percent of the money they raised each year to National; the more money you raised, the more you contributed. Also, many of the larger affiliates voluntarily contributed an additional $10,000 annually as part of the Chairman's Challenge. We felt the money we provided was not insignificant, so to be cut out of a major decision like changing the name and mission of the organization didn't sit well with us.

Considering this rebellion had been born and had seen some of its finest hours in a hotel bar, our setting Friday night helped us fall back in step with one another easily. Over drinks and dinner, we reminisced, shared personal stories, and rehashed the conference. By the time we reconvened at 8:00 the next morning over coffee and pastries in the meeting room, we were ready to get to work.

The question we were struggling with was whether we should begin a new national organization. The agenda of the daylong session had been set by our facilitator, Mary Ann Probicki. She asked us to answer five questions: What is the perceived purpose or mission for a national organization? What programs/services and functions would it pursue? What resources and structure would be needed to perform these functions? What engagement by others in partnerships would be required? What steps would need to be taken in research, planning, and communications?

"Before we get started, I'm going to set some ground rules," she announced. "I would like to call you all to 'conscious attention.'" Unsure what that meant, I noticed myself and others around the room sitting up straighter and putting down our muffins.

"When Judy Bannon hired me to be your facilitator for this meeting, she told me that emotions have been running high in light of SIDS Alliance's transition to First Candle. However, today we focus on the future, not the past." Heads nodded in understanding.

"We must be accountable to this process and to the people involved here. You've already followed the first ground rule, which is to show up. So, welcome! The rest of the ground rules are pay attention; tell the truth as you know it; and, perhaps most importantly, do not be wedded to an outcome prematurely. Jumping ahead to planning the structure of this organization before understanding if the organization is needed, and what its ultimate purpose should be, is a flawed approach. Let's take one step at a time."

Initially, I had been unsure if using a facilitator was absolutely necessary. Would she really be worth the money we were paying? When I had made contact with her, she had known little about the SIDS movement, but it was clear she'd done her homework since then. The ground rules were a good sign, too. Having someone outside the situation running things, someone with no emotion invested in the outcome, seemed key. Aside from that, she was skilled at keeping us focused on our goals, which was crucial considering the brief time we had together, from 8:00 a.m. to 5:00 p.m. that day.

First, Mary Ann got us thinking about what the mission of this new organization should be. We brainstormed words and phrases we felt represented the identity of the initiative and its purpose. She clarified for us that purpose can be thought of as "reason for existence" and shouldn't be confused with "activity" or "program." A purpose defines the long-term commitment of the organization, not the activities it might engage in to fulfill that commitment.

We then broke into four small groups and began drafting rough mission statements using the words from the brainstorm. When we shared our statements, we found common language and ideas, which didn't surprise us. We worked together to incorporate our thoughts into one working mission statement that read: "XYZ is a national partnership of SIDS advocates whose mission is to promote infant survival and grief support for those affected by a sudden infant death." This process took some time. Each word was carefully considered. Identifying the entity as a "partnership" was meant to convey a spirit of cooperation among equal SIDS advocates rather than a hierarchy. We envisioned a "national" entity because the group members agreed that there was a clear need to connect local SIDS organizations throughout the country. The verb "promote" was chosen to clarify that the organization would advocate for other agents, not provide a direct service. Mary Ann urged us to think carefully before committing to the dual purpose of infant survival and grief support. While we understood that splitting our focus in this way would be more challenging, we knew all too well that the effort toward infant survival is not always successful and that support for grieving families requires specialized attention. After some discussion we agreed that promoting the sharing of resources, rather than managing them, was more fitting. While we considered education and research key to the promotion of infant survival and grief support, we didn't explicitly include them in the statement because they fell into the category of "activities" and not "reason for existence."

The area of greatest need seemed to be making expertise and quality resources available in areas where none currently existed. While there were many SIDS agencies throughout the country, there was no visible leadership pulling them together and expanding their capacity to serve the needs of their communities. We considered this function to be significant enough that we added it to the mission statement, which was changed to read: "XYZ is a national partnership of SIDS advocates whose mission is *to provide leadership in* the promotion of infant survival and grief support for those affected by a sudden infant death."

Now that we had a clearly defined mission, we could see that there were two potential directions this organization could take and that each would need a different structure. The first direction was to provide leadership to facilitate and coordinate SIDS resources, materials, programs, and services on a national level. The other direction was to act as a watchdog agency monitoring already existing SIDS organizations. To help us choose our path, we agreed that the group would research the roles, functions, and structures of these organizations.

We felt energized after the morning session, feeling that we'd made incredible progress in just a few short hours. We worked through lunch, eating while brainstorming the functions we felt the new entity should perform. We decided on facilitating and co-ordinating the expanded use of materials, resources, and people to make them more broadly available across the United States; creating new educational materials and programs; and providing leadership to the SIDS community.

Judy Rainey and I sat together at the conference table discussing Cribs for Kids during the afternoon break. She wanted to know everything we were do-ing—how the process was working, what our results had been, how we were funding it, and so on. Once everyone was seated and ready to resume the meeting, she spoke right up, which has always been her style. "What are we doing here? We have a program. It's called Cribs for Kids. Judy Bannon's already doing it." I didn't know if I should hug her or shush her.

"People in Michigan have cribs," one rep from Michigan SIDS Alliance answered. I doubted that could be said of everyone in the state. Even as an out-sider, I knew of the poverty in areas like Detroit and Flint. Quickly realizing that she wouldn't get far argu-ing the demographics of Michigan with a resident of that state, though, Judy tried a different tack.

"Well, that's not enough. Cribs for Kids isn't just a crib giveaway; it's educational, too. We need to teach them that they have to *use their cribs.*"

Mary Ann, who could see the potential this topic had for throwing us deeply off schedule, steered us back on track. I dutifully followed.

Next on the agenda was the task of generating a list of needed structures and resources. These mostly centered on communication and visibility—for instance, procuring a 1-800 number; creating a logo, standard educational materials, and a website; and determining human-resource needs (volunteers, staff, spokesperson, etc.). Finally, we had to determine criteria for partnership and funding streams.

We began to look at two organizational models. The first was a loose-knit association or network model. This choice offered flexibility but might not have sufficient strength to provide any significant leadership or impact. The second model was the traditional 501(c)3 nonprofit incorporation model. This structure would be required if we wanted to receive grant and donation funding. The drawback was its complexity—requiring a board, officers, and bylaws at the very least. Operating under another nonprofit corporation as our fiduciary agent would eliminate the challenge of creating a 501(c)3, but it would place us under the authority of that agent. Since none of these models were without cons, we decided to research other possible models before making a decision.

To help further our understanding of our structural needs, we had to define if we were creating an entity of members or partners. A membership structure would have varying levels of involvement and would require dues to support programs. Members would be expected to contribute to the efforts of the organization on a somewhat consistent basis and would have a stake in the organization's mission and success. In contrast, a partnership would engage partners in collaborative arrangements as time and projects required. The sense of the group was that both structures were needed for different reasons.

We decided that creating a list of agencies who would potentially participate in the organization might help us further define the differences between partners and members. We quickly saw that most of the identified groups were placed in the partner column, not the member column, though some were placed in both. The partner column included national organizations such as the American Academy of Pediatrics (AAP), National Institutes of Health (NIH), Association of SIDS and Infant Mortality Programs (ASIP), and CJ Foundation for SIDS (CJ), while the member column consisted of SIDS-specific organizations, SIDS Alliance affiliates, and bereavement programs such as Compassionate Friends and SHARE. We found that members tended to focus on SIDS programs and services and had missions similar to the one we had developed, while partners had a broader focus, with SIDS being only a part of their mission. We considered the idea that individual persons within some "partner" organizations might become members.

As we talked, we realized that many of the potential partners on our list had similar functions to the national entity we were looking to create. (ASIP and CJ were specifically cited.) Was a professional association actually needed? Why create something that already exists and have to compete against more established groups? Perhaps a watchdog organization would be a more effective use of our time. A group of this nature would still fulfill our mission statement. However, it would have to be structured much differently than what we had initially proposed.

We also agreed that all the organizations represented at the meeting would formally disaffiliate from SIDS Alliance (now First Candle) and would communicate this action to other affiliates. Transparency was important to us so that there would be no perception that we supported the change to First Candle. Also, we wanted to let other affiliates know of our plans in case they were interested in participating in the new entity.

By this time, our day was ending. We assigned each member of the group a research role to fulfill before our next meeting in the spring. Some would look into the missions, functions, and structures of existing national SIDS organizations; others would study the organizational structures of existing advocacy and watchdog groups.

As I drove home, I found myself thinking about the mission statement we'd arrived at—"XYZ is a national partnership of SIDS advocates whose mission is to provide leadership in the promotion of infant survival and grief support for those affected by a sudden infant death." *Cribs for Kids fits that mission.* Then I began considering everything else we'd discussed—organizational structures, revenue streams, staffing—and pushed the thought from my mind.

A few weeks later, I attended a SIDS conference in Washington, DC, along with a few of the people who had attended the Pittsburgh meeting. Barry Bornstein, executive director of the CJ Foundation for SIDS, was also there. CJ is an organization started in 1994 by Joel and Susan Hollander after the death of their daughter, Carly Jenna, and has been, since its inception, one of the largest SIDS organizations in the country. Joel, who was the CEO of Westwood One when his daughter died, had a close relationship with radio personality Don Imus at WFAN in New York City. Imus was so saddened by Carly's death that he proposed the newly formed CJ Foundation for SIDS to be the recipient of WFAN's Fourth Annual Radiothon to raise money for SIDS research. That one event raised $1.4 million, getting CJ off to an auspicious start. Aside from funding research, CJ also sponsors various grant programs and had funded many of our SIDS affiliates at one time or another.

Word had gotten back to Barry that a group of SIDS Alliance affiliates were planning to secede and start their own national organization. At the end of the first day of the conference, he asked if those of us who had been part of the Pittsburgh meeting could join him in the hotel lobby for a short meeting.

"I've had an epiphany!" he declared when we all had gathered. "Why go through all of the red tape of creating a new 501(c)3? You don't want to do that. You're going to have to create a board of directors, and there's so much paperwork. You should all become partners of CJ, and our board can oversee what you're doing. That way you can keep moving forward with your SIDS work and not get sidetracked."

CJ had never been interested in having partners or members previously. However, I supposed that they found creating a partnership preferable to having to compete against another national organization. Plus, taking on the seceding SIDS Alliance affiliates would make CJ the largest SIDS organization in the United States. Since we all had the same goal, why not join forces? Barry set up a conference call with Judy Rainey, Nancy Maruyama (executive director of education and community services at SIDS of Illinois and a participant at our Pittsburgh meeting), and me on March 18, 2003, so that we could discuss his offer further.

On the conference call, Barry told us that CJ was prepared to welcome partners who were independent organizations with a focus on SIDS or other infant deaths and who subscribed to the partnership's mission. (The mission statement would be created at a later time.) This meant we would have to resign our interests in First Candle, which was not a problem since we had resolved to do that at our February meeting. Adding "CJ" to our organizations' names wasn't deemed necessary.

The benefits of becoming a partner were having CJ as a brokerage, clearinghouse system, and liaison between local organizations. They pledged to create an advisory group to help facilitate communication between partners and send out weekly e-mail updates. They would also support the partnership through operating grants and research funding.

The group who had met in February reconvened in Pittsburgh on June 7. On the table was Barry's proposal to take us on as partners. After some initial discussion, it was agreed that joining forces with CJ was a viable option. However, we didn't want to give up all of our power. We had learned our lesson from dealing with National, and we wanted to control our own fates going forward. To that end, we spent the day coming up with our own list of criteria and expectations for this joint venture. We felt it was important to consider this a pilot project with an evaluation after one year to assess if the partnership was allowing us to accomplish our goals. At that point we could decide on a future direction. We agreed that our Year One Advisory/Steering Committee would be composed of representatives from our largest organizations—Michigan, Ohio, Illinois, and Pennsylvania—and partnership should only be open to organizations with 501(c)3s and full-time executive directors. So that entities who did not meet partnership criteria were not entirely excluded, we decided to create short-term work teams for nonpartners.

As our national partner, we would expect CJ to foster relationships with national and local sponsors. We would look to them to make connections to media; provide press releases, brochures, PSAs, and a newsletter template; and maintain a website and listserv. We also expected them to create a part-time position for a liaison to coordinate communication, activities, and mailings between national and local partners.

By the end of the day, we had voted yes, and the CJ Foundation for SIDS Partnership was born, consisting of representatives from Illinois, Michigan, Ohio, Oklahoma, Pennsylvania, SIDS Mid-Atlantic, and Washington State.

• • •

At the same time that we began focusing on this new partnership, interest in Cribs for Kids started to boil over. In March 2003, the *Pittsburgh Tribune-Review* published an article detailing how Cribs for Kids was being "credited by local and national officials with dramatically lowering SIDS deaths in Allegheny County." From 1997 to 2001, our rates had dropped 60 percent. At the date of publication, it had been eight months since the area had seen a SIDS death. We'd given out about 2,200 cribs at that point in Allegheny and neighboring Westmoreland County, and all the babies who'd received them had celebrated their first birthdays.

I was traveling throughout the state speaking at conferences, hospitals, and community meetings, teaching safe-sleep practices to anyone who would listen. Thrilled to have solid statistics to back up our anecdotal evidence, I shared them during every talk. The response Cribs for Kids received was gratifying. Audiences were inspired by the fact that providing education and cribs could save so many lives. After every talk, people would approach me and ask, "Can you provide this service in our community?" Just as I was unable to say no to the mothers who called our offices looking for assistance, I couldn't deny these requests either. However, I had to be realistic about our limitations. So I answered, "We don't have the resources to expand right now, but I can teach you how to do what we do." I was surprised by how many people accepted the challenge. Over the phone and via e-mail, I would guide them through the process—finding a crib vendor, appealing to low-income mothers—and would send them safe-sleep brochures in the mail. The start-up money and logistical demands involved in taking Cribs for Kids nationwide were as elusive as ever in spite of the goodwill of local funders, like District 3 of the Pennsylvania Business and Professional Women's Club, who'd gifted us with $5,600 at a time when funds were particularly scarce, coming forward to support us. This method of sharing our resources seemed like a workable solution until I could figure out something better.

It was at one of these speaking engagements that I met neonatologist Dr. Michael Goodstein, who is now Cribs for Kids' medical director of research and one of our most impassioned and dogged supporters. Connecting with Mike at this critical time in our development is one of our most enduring success stories. "I went from rolling my eyes at having to sit through a lecture about cribs to being a fervent believer in the course of one presentation," he says.

That presentation was at WellSpan York Hospital. I had been invited to present at grand rounds by Dr. David Turkewitz, chairman of the Department of Pediatrics, who had heard me speak at the statewide Child Death Review conference. He felt it imperative that his staff be educated about safe sleep. After I spoke about our program and drop in SIDS rates, Dr. Turkewitz told his assembled staff, "I believe in this program, but I'm going to need help with it. I have too much on my plate now. Is there anyone here who can help me?"

In the back of the room, a hand shot up immediately. It belonged to Mike. The way he tells the story is as follows:

"I almost didn't go to the lecture. I had been on call the night before and was exhausted. When I saw the topic, I thought, *What do I need to know about cribs? Everybody puts their baby in one, right?* Apparently not. So, as I'm walking out the door, I'm pulled back by this great, powerful force called Jewish guilt. In my head I can hear my mother's voice saying, 'Michael, go to the lecture. Learn something!' Who can argue with that? I went to the lecture.

"Judy always likes to say I was sitting in the back of the room, but I always sit in the second row! So, once she gets done blowing us away with her decreased mortality statistics, David Turkewitz says we can do this in York. I'm thinking, *Fifty dollars for a Pack 'n Play to save a baby's life? How can I say no?* I was sick of being heartbroken, getting called down to the Emergency Department to try to resuscitate these babies who had died of this horrible tragedy. It is life altering to do that, working over a beautiful, previously healthy baby, very much loved, with family members by your side as you are doing chest compressions. There was no doubt that I was in. I raised my hand and said I would help. Please note the word *help*. I wasn't planning on being in charge. But I kept pestering Dr. Turkewitz, thinking I was missing meetings because no one was contacting me about getting the ball rolling with Cribs for Kids. Finally he said that he was just too busy to lead the charge and asked me to take over.

"I had never done anything like this, so I said I'd do it if he helped me. We formed a committee and did some research on our local rates and needs, and Judy helped me write a grant to the Young Women's Club, which brought us about $3,000. Judy told me that Ronald McDonald House had not only given her a grant but had awarded grants of $5,000 to several other groups who were taking part in the Cribs for Kids campaign. I remember calling her a few months later to break the news that I did not get $5,000 from them. She immediately tried to soothe my hurt feelings with sympathetic words. When I finally got a word in, I told her, 'They gave me $7,500!' We immediately had a run of sleep deaths in York. Luckily, we were financially prepared to open up shop right away. We haven't looked back."

A few months later, our group gathered for our third meeting in Pittsburgh. We discussed what the focus of our partnership with CJ should be. Feeling we needed something to distinguish us from other SIDS organizations, we went back to the notes from the first meeting, reviewing our mission statement and revisiting conversations about organizational structures. Judy Rainey was not able to attend the meeting, but she and I had had many conversations about the partnership's focus. On one of our calls, she said, "Why are we struggling to find a direction to take? We know that putting babies in cribs can save lives, so that's what we should focus on. Look at the mission statement. It describes Cribs for Kids!" I didn't tell her that I had been thinking the same thing. "You have partners all over, whether you call them that or not, who are following your model for providing safe-sleep education and distributing cribs. Leadership—the whole concept of safe sleep and putting babies in cribs is new, so that means Cribs for Kids is leading the way. Infant survival—look at your rates. They're lower than anyone's. What's left? Grief support. Well, Cribs for Kids has that covered too, although if we champion Cribs for Kids like we should, hopefully grief support will become unnecessary."

What Judy had said about partners was true. Until that moment I'd viewed our inability to service the whole country as a shortcoming; I had thought the act of sharing Cribs for Kids' methods was a stopgap until we could figure out how to expand. It reminds me of the John Lennon quote, "Life is what happens when you're busy making other plans." I was so busy trying to figure out how to expand Cribs for Kids that I didn't realize that Cribs for Kids was expanding every time I invited someone else to follow our model.

So at that third meeting, with Judy's words echoing in my mind, I spoke up about focusing the partnership on safe sleep and Cribs for Kids. I looked around the room and saw that my colleagues were nodding their heads, amenable to the idea. They were already actively educating their communities about safe sleep. Now they would become Cribs for Kids partners and begin distributing cribs too.

That Monday I got to work creating the Cribs for Kids Toolkit, a binder of twenty-six documents that were necessary for setting up a Cribs for Kids program. These documents ranged from safe-sleep materials to legal forms. I sent toolkits to everyone who'd been at the meeting that weekend and set some aside in anticipation of further growth. On our website we invited interested parties to e-mail us about becoming partners and added instructions on our phone system directing people to dial my extension to discuss the opportunity. I began to actively recruit new partners at my speaking engagements, too. The toolkit made the whole process so simple, and our only expenses were postage, paper, and binders. Pretty soon we were adding new partners every week. The safe-sleep message was spreading, and our partners were taking on the responsibility of procuring cribs for mothers in their areas. Since these partners already had relationships with their local health departments and foundations, they were in a better position than we would have been to approach them for funding. With the *Trib* article touting our plummeting rates in hand, they were able to show that Cribs for Kids was worthy of support.

Our physicist friends from the beginning of the chapter have another teaching; this one is definite enough to be considered a law. They tell us that for every action there is an equal and opposite reaction. It seems that holds true in the theoretical world of nonprofits as well as in the natural world. Cribs for Kids' rapid growth led to the dissolution of the CJ Foundation for SIDS Partnership in less than a year. Our group of disgruntled affiliates had gotten into the partnership so that we didn't have to start our own national organization. Once Cribs for Kids' partner base began reaching across the country, we had to question our need for the CJ partnership. It felt like our work with CJ was running on a parallel track to Cribs for Kids. It wasn't enhancing our growth, nor had it been designed to. In 2004 we parted ways with CJ. All of our allies from the Pittsburgh meetings remained with Cribs for Kids.

Bob O'Connor had some concerns with our new model. He felt that if we were going to share our materials and methods, we needed to require partners to sign an agreement defining their obligations and benefits. He also felt we needed to copyright our name and trademark our logo. To this end, he set up a meeting for me at Thorp, Reed and Armstrong, a prestigious Pittsburgh law firm. They began the process of copyrighting the name "Cribs for Kids" and creating a trademark license agreement that interested parties would sign, *officially* making them partners. Signing the license agreement entitled them to access to all of our materials, as well as guidance in implementing the program. Becoming a Cribs for Kids partner wouldn't supersede any other affiliations or identities they already had. If they desired, they could remain independent organizations with their own names and missions. However, insofar as they provided safe-sleep education and cribs, they would follow the tenets of our program, use our materials with our logo and name, and give credit to Cribs for Kids.

While our lawyers were working out the legalities, we continued to unofficially recruit partners. A large social-service organization on the East Coast requested that I speak to their board of directors about starting a Cribs for Kids program. Initially this seemed like a great opportunity, but it wasn't long before their representative was calling me with various complaints and suggestions. Before I knew it, I was receiving calls from one of their funders, speaking on their behalf.

"Well, how about if I set up a meeting halfway between our two locations, and we can hash this all out?" he asked me at one point.

"There's nothing to hash out," I told him. "This is my program. I don't have to change it for anyone. If they don't like the way Cribs for Kids works, they don't have to be a partner. They can create their own materials and give out cribs themselves."

I felt that I was rather direct, but soon after that, I found myself on a conference call with the organization's executive director and the funder. Together they tried to convince me to sign a "memorandum of understanding." They even offered to have their attorneys draw it up. I didn't know what a memorandum of understanding was, but I suspected that since their attorney was drawing it up, it had something to do with trying to wrestle control of Cribs for Kids from me.

"Well, we're not happy with this logo. We have an idea for a new logo," I was told.

"That's our identity. We're not going to have two logos," I answered.

"Also, this isn't the playard we want to distribute. We want to give out the Simplicity brand."

"You're welcome to provide a different safe-sleep environment and create your own logo; you just can't call your program Cribs for Kids if you do."

That's when it hit me that our name was the sticking point. That's what all of this endless back and forth had been about. Cribs for Kids was becoming a brand, a name that meant something to people. This woman wanted to do things *her* way, but she wanted to use *our* name. Her thinking had been flawed twice. First, she thought she could push me around, making changes and exerting her influence, until eventually she was in control of my program. Clearly, I wasn't going to let that happen. Second, she assumed we hadn't been savvy enough to secure the program legally. Bob's instincts had been right on the money.

"Actually, I can call it Cribs for Kids if I'd like. You don't have a copyright on that name. I had my lawyers look into it." The paperwork had already been filed, so while the copyright wasn't official yet, legally we already had rights to the name. Her lawyers, of course, would have had no way to know that.

Because this is a book, you'll think this next part is fiction, but I promise it isn't. It's the hand of God. Right at that moment, Michaelleene walked into my office with the mail and put a manila envelope from the attorney's office on my desk. I tore it open and smiled.

"*Actually,* I have the legal documents right here. How about if I fax them to you?"

I put the two of them on hold and rushed to the other room, reading each sheet as fast as I could before feeding it into the fax machine.

By the time I returned to the phone, the pages were printing out in their offices, being read as quickly as they had been at my end, I'm sure.

"Trademark license agreement, copyrights, trademarks? Why did you think you had to go to these extremes?" they were sputtering just before hanging up their phones.

The next day I sent out the agreement to everyone who was using the program, inviting them to become our first official partners. All the documents were returned to us, signed, within a few weeks, giving Cribs for Kids a presence in seven states. We were finally on our way to becoming a national organization.

On the surface it might seem funny that we found the solution to our expansion problem while focused on a different problem, but if you pay attention, you'll notice that is how life (or is it the hand of God?) often works. Ever have a lightbulb moment in the shower or wake up remembering the old friend's name that had eluded you the night before? Of course, we all have. Have you ever solved a problem in the middle of the night while your mind was racing, and you just wished you could fall back asleep? Probably not. If you're like me, all you manage to do in those moments is think of fifteen more problems.

Our conscious brains stop us from finding answers for many reasons. Sometimes we think we already know the answer, and it's an answer we don't like or aren't ready to accept. I was questioning how to make Cribs for Kids a viable national entity. The one answer my conscious brain knew involved an intimidating amount of time and money. Frustrated, I put that problem aside and focused on the CJ/SIDS partnership and running Cribs for Kids locally. I stopped thinking about *how* to expand Cribs for Kids, but I kept picturing in my mind what the rates would look like if all low-income mothers had cribs and used them properly. I pictured safe sleep being taught in hospitals and doctor's offices around the country, becoming as common a practice as Back to Sleep. I pictured moms everywhere putting their babies down in clean, uncluttered cribs. I pictured those babies growing into toddlers, teens, adults. It was my dream, and dreams don't go away just because we tell them to. They sneak in while we're driving, showering, sleeping, grocery shopping, vacuuming, gardening—pretty much anytime we have that faraway look in our eyes. Thank God they're such sneaks, because those visions are where all the power lies—as long as you don't kill them with the *hows.* "How do I get what I want?" is much too open-ended and often leads to the three words we're most uncomfortable with: "I don't know." If we could all get better with "I don't know," then "how" would be OK, too. But until that day comes, we have to stick with "*What* do I want?" You know what you want. Picture it. Talk about it. Draw it. Sing and dance about it if you like. Most importantly, embrace it. Let the power of *what* figure out *how* while you're busy making other plans.

Lesson 5

● ● ●

ASK FOR AND ACCEPT HELP.

*Let us not seek the Republican
answer or the Democratic
answer, but the right answer.*

—*John F. Kennedy*

I grew up in a mill town about fifteen miles south of
Pittsburgh called Clairton. My father worked for US
Steel at Clairton Works as a crane operator. In 1961,
when he died of lymphoma caused by the dangerous
working conditions in which he toiled, I was fifteen.
He was forty-three. During the last autumn he was
with us, the country was caught up in the drama of the
1960 election. Having never had a president who wasn't

a grandfather type, my best friends Sue and Noreen and I were fascinated by the possibility of the youthful, fashionable Kennedys ascending to the White House. The senator was making a campaign stop in Pittsburgh, so we hopped on the bus and headed downtown to see if we could meet him. We felt confident since we had successfully tracked down Bobby Darin in his hotel on a similar mission a few months earlier, finding out his room number by following the bellman whom we'd overheard being asked to "deliver this fruit basket to Mr. Darin's room." Upon the bellman's departure, we knocked on the door and eventually left with not just his autograph but that of his girlfriend, Sandra Dee. We used the same strategy in our pursuit of Kennedy, spending the afternoon loitering in and around the historic William Penn Hotel, where we assumed he was staying. Our perseverance was rewarded when one of his aides came spinning through the revolving door and, finding three pretty high-school girls peeking out from behind the cabstand, stuck "Kennedy for President" signs in our hands and stationed us by a limousine idling at the curb.

We were not the only members of the farewell committee—crowds of spectators were lined up across the street behind police barricades—but we had the best vantage point, standing next to Governor David L. Lawrence and District Attorney Edward C. Boyle under the hotel's front awning. The two men, politicians who were skilled at making small talk, engaged us in conversation, and we, too young and inexperienced to feel nervous, chatted away with them. In fact, we felt so comfortable conversing with the DA that when he said, "Anytime you're downtown, you should come to my office and visit me," we never considered not obliging him. I can still remember walking into the waiting area of his office in the Allegheny County Courthouse and greeting his secretary, who would jump on the intercom and say, "Mr. Boyle, the girls are here." A moment later, his office door would open, and a couple of lawyers in expensive suits would walk out to take our places in the waiting area as we filed inside. He was a rotund man who would sit with his hands on his belly and listen to us rattle on about our lives, probably the only insight he had to the lives of teenagers in the '60s.

When the senator exited the hotel, he shook each of our hands, exclaiming, "I see we have some very pretty guests with us today," in that trademark Harvard accent. Our focus on him was complete, so we never noticed my older sister, Diane, who was across the street trying to break through the police line to get to us.

"I have to get in there. That's my sister!" she told the officer blocking her way.

"Honey, right now she's everybody's sister," was his droll reply.

"But she has my white blazer on!" she told him, as if that piece of evidence would be the clincher.

It may not have carried much weight with the cop, but it vindicated me at home that night where I breathlessly told the tale of my brush with greatness to my three younger siblings, Beverly, Teri and Danny, and my doubtful parents. "Judy, are you sure you're telling us the truth?" they asked incredulously. I feared they would never believe me, until Diane bounded into the house shouting, "Judy borrowed my white blazer without asking again!" At this point, I was in my pajamas, so I knew it was my word against hers.

"I did not!" I insisted.

"I know she did! I saw her downtown! She was shaking Senator Kennedy's hand, and she had on *my* white blazer!" For once, I happily let her win the argument.

One of the last memories I have of Daddy was how much he laughed that night as my story came full circle. He died three and a half months later. We missed him furiously, our strong, youthful father whose life was cut short by the harsh working conditions of the mill, who fought for change walking picket lines as often as he brought home a paycheck. He and Kennedy were both born in 1917. Kennedy was inaugurated on January 20, 1961. Daddy died January 31. We watched the president's star rise after Daddy's had so recently fallen and thought we'd found in this leader some of what we'd lost—youth, idealism, the power to take care of us and protect us from harm. Soon JFK's portrait graced our wall next to Grandma's framed photo of the pope, and each Sunday morning on our knees, we followed our priest in thanking God for his leadership.

Clearly, being a Republican was never in the cards for me.

Once we had our trademark license agreement in place, I felt an even greater responsibility to make Cribs for Kids a success. We were making a play to put ourselves at the forefront of the safe-sleep movement, and if we couldn't score, we'd better take a seat on the bench. The work that needed to be done was too important.

My oldest daughter, Kelly, had just gotten engaged. Her future in-laws, Joe and Pat James, invited us to their Squirrel Hill home one bright Sunday afternoon to sit on their deck, sip cocktails, and talk wedding plans. At the time Joe was the Allegheny County Common Pleas president judge and knew many of the political players in Pennsylvania.

"How's that crib program going?" he asked once talk of seating charts, meal choices, and deejays waned.

"The longer we keep at it, the greater the need grows. We're constantly searching for funding," I told him.

"Why don't you approach Senator Santorum?"

"I can't even get into his office," I answered. There were plenty of advantages to having heavy hitters representing your state in the US Senate, but accessibility wasn't one of them.

"Well, he's prolife. I'd think he'd be interested in showing he cares about babies once they're born, too," he said. "I have breakfast with his staff every Tuesday morning. Let me see what I can do. Call me Tuesday afternoon."

For a dyed-in-the-wool liberal like me, approaching Rick Santorum, a staunchly right-wing politician, felt hypocritical. Not only hadn't I voted for him, I couldn't see myself ever voting for him, regardless of what help he might provide Cribs for Kids. The more I thought about it, though, the more I realized that was a foolish line of thinking. My responsibility wasn't to myself or to him; it was to babies without safe places to sleep. Furthermore, Senator Santorum was my senator, whether I had voted for him or not, and I was his constituent. I decided to accept Joe's help in setting up a meeting.

Within a week I was in the senator's offices in South Side, about twenty blocks from ours, in the Landmarks Building. The building was built in 1900 as the Pittsburgh Terminal Train Station, and the common spaces retained an old-world charm. Refined touches like the cornice and wrought-iron grillwork of the elevators made a grand impression. Santorum's suite was utilitarian, however, filled with neutral-colored cubicles like any corporate environment.

My meeting was with Keith Schmidt, the senator's state director. He was not a cubicle dweller. He had a posh office with a massive oak desk and large windows that allowed light to shine in from behind as he worked. I sat down across from him, leaning forward, ankles crossed as the sisters had taught me at St. Elizabeth's a million years earlier. He leaned back in his chair and kicked his feet up on his desk, arms crossed. The message was clear—I was in the room because of whom I knew. I needed to make an impression fast before I was politely shuffled out the door.

I launched into the story of Cribs for Kids—how we'd gotten started and what had kept us going up to this point. Schmidt was restless when he interrupted my pitch and said, "So, what would you like the senator to do?"

I figured this was my chance to make an impression, for better or for worse. "Well, the scuttlebutt is that the senator is prolife, but he doesn't care much about what happens to babies once they're born."

He looked at me incredulously, probably unable to believe my nerve. To be honest, I had surprised myself.

"Who says that?" he asked.

"Everyone," I answered simply. He put his feet on the floor. I continued my story, this time with his full attention. I could see the wheels turning in his mind.

When I was done talking, he called down the hall, "Randy!"

A handsome kid in his twenties bounded into the room.

"Tell Randy the story you just told me," he said, and then he turned around and began feverishly typing an e-mail.

Randy was Randy Vulakovich, Jr., a young man from Shaler Township, a suburb of Pittsburgh. He was bright and enthusiastic, and he asked me a number of insightful questions. At one point, Keith turned around and read his e-mail aloud to me.

"Does that sound factually correct? Is it what you just told me?" I confirmed that it was and noticed that it was addressed to the senator with a subject line that read *priority*. "I want you to meet with him face-to-face. I can tell him this story, but I think it will be more effective if you do. You've got the passion to sell it," he told me.

We met at the Duquesne Club, a storied establishment in Downtown Pittsburgh that has catered to the business elite since 1873. Its early members included Andrew Carnegie, George Westinghouse, and Henry Clay Frick. Needless to say, having a breakfast meeting there with a US senator isn't your average workday experience. I asked Jim Agras, who was not only one of our most loyal board members but a prominent local Republican, to accompany me. We arrived promptly and were led into a lavish yet cozy room appointed with sumptuous overstuffed chairs, polished coffee tables, and plush carpeting. The wood-paneled walls emitted a warm sheen and were dotted here and there with built-in bookshelves and tasteful oil paintings. Because of the early hour, the room was mostly empty, making it easy for us to spot the senator, who was seated in one of the comfortable chairs drinking coffee and reading the paper. He rose when we approached, shook our hands, and invited us to sit on a couch opposite him. I was glad I'd brought Jim with me. He was taking this scene in stride, but I was intimidated. I remembered the days when women were not even permitted inside the Duquesne Club. In the mid-1960s, I was the secretary to the president of US Steel, Edwin H. Gott. One year the club made an exception to this discriminatory rule on his behalf and agreed to allow him to host a Christmas luncheon there for his staff. I felt simultaneously thrilled and sickened by the special treatment and smuggled home a couple of their ornate champagne glasses in a spontaneous moment of rebellion. I guess they were right; they shouldn't have let me in.

The senator was dressed in an immaculate suit with a red silk tie and a red rubber bracelet (of the Livestrong variety) on his left wrist. I wondered what cause the bracelet championed and flashed briefly on a day when he might wear one for Cribs for Kids. He was professional, dispensing of small talk after a short time and plunging into the business at hand. I was impressed by his knowledge of Cribs for Kids and could tell his staff had given thought to how he might benefit us. Because he is the father of seven children, he knew all about Pack 'n Plays, too.

"Where do you get the product?" he asked.

I told him about our arrangement with Toys "R" Us.

"No, you have to get them directly from the manufacturer. Are they Graco?"

I told him they were.

"Graco Children's Products is located in Pennsylvania. I'll get you in touch with their president, Howard Heckes, and tell him you want to be a distributor. Then you can get them at cost and supply your partners. Of course, you'll need a warehouse."

I sat there nodding my head. "Of course." I knew better than to say anything that might sound like I was uncertain. Now wasn't the time to ask questions. Now was the time to say yes. He took my card and assured me that I would be hearing back from his team. "This is an example of a perfect public-private partnership," he beamed.

Within a week, a letter from his office appeared on my desk, addressed to Howard Heckes, cc'd to me, telling Mr. Heckes that the senator requested he meet with me to talk about the future of Cribs for Kids.

Two weeks after that, I was making the five-and-a-half-hour drive from Pittsburgh to Graco's corporate headquarters in Exton, Pennsylvania. I arrived at a four-story building that sat alone on the side of the highway. Before entering, I took a moment in the car to freshen up and take a few deep breaths, reviewing in my mind the key points that I wanted to make during the meeting. I walked through the doors into an atrium lobby with balconies circling the interior on all four levels. Displays of cribs, Pack 'n Plays, strollers, and swings took away any doubt that I'd found the right place.

I assumed that Howard Heckes would be an older man, silver-haired, in a conservative, blue-pinstriped suit. I was surprised when I learned he was the fortyish man wearing a golf shirt who greeted me when I entered the waiting area. He immediately put me at ease with his easygoing manner.

"It isn't often that I get a request from a US senator to take a meeting with someone." I smiled, liking the footing the introduction had put me on.

He escorted me to a conference room where his marketing team was assembled, eager to strategize how this public-private partnership could benefit us all. I was gratified when I realized that they already seemed to be sold on the idea. All that was left for me to do was to prove that I could really pull it off.

After giving them the overview of our program, I shifted the conversation to their interests. "I'm sure it's obvious what the advantage is to my organization, so let's talk about how it would benefit Graco," I began. "First, the women who will be receiving free product are not your customers. If they could afford to buy Pack 'n Plays, they would. This is an opportunity to provide assistance to women and babies who really need it without taking away potential profit from you. Second, through this program we can turn the Graco Pack 'n Play from a playpen where a baby can sleep in a pinch into a legitimate safe-sleep environment. Playpens are optional equipment. In fact, they're often frowned upon these days. But every baby needs a safe place to sleep. There was a time when we provided full-sized cribs to our mothers to mixed reviews. Once we started providing Pack 'n Plays, we received nothing but raves. They're easy to assemble, and they travel easily wherever the baby goes. Once we start distributing these throughout the country, your product goes from being an option to being an essential item."

I knew I had them when they started talking about how they could keep the cost down for us. We discussed creating a special Cribs for Kids model of the Pack 'n Play that could be altered cosmetically to lower the manufacturing price. Someone suggested we could use leftover bolts of fabric from previous seasons in gender-neutral colors.

"We can remove the toy bar," I offered. The current model came equipped with a semicircular bar with toys hanging from it that arced over the baby, like a mobile. This bar came with a warning sticker telling parents to remove it once the baby was five months old. "Our program is all about safety. We can't include an item with a warning sticker on it."

It was also decided our model would have its own SKU number so it couldn't be returned to retail stores for cash or store credit, only back to our organization.

We were on a roll, ideas flowing, spirits high, when talk turned to me procuring a warehouse to handle the product. I found myself growing anxious again, putting on my best face to mask my ignorance.

"You'll have to order entire containers of the product in order for this to be financially feasible. That's one thousand five hundred and thirteen Pack 'n Plays in each order. Do you think that will be a problem?"

"No, not at all. We can make that work."

"Great. Probably what will happen is they'll come into the Port of Los Angeles, where we'll pick them up by truck or take them by rail into Pittsburgh…"

Driving home on the turnpike, my mind was spinning between euphoria and fear. I knew that this was a turning point. All this time I had been looking for someone to buy cribs for us, when the answer was for us to be the provider. If we orchestrated this right, we would no longer be dependent on grants or fund-raising; we'd have a product to sell, giving us the potential to make all the money that we needed to grow Cribs for Kids throughout the country. The problem was that in order to make this happen, we were going to have to lay out $57,000 to buy a container of cribs, not to mention figuring out where to store them and how to ship them. To say there was a learning curve was an understatement. This was a learning spiral, curve upon curve upon curve, and I wasn't sure if I was on an upward spin or drilling myself straight into the ground.

We spent the next couple months negotiating prices and configuring a shipping model with Graco. Although they were happy to be involved in a worthwhile charitable enterprise, they aren't a charity. The bottom line was going to have to remain within certain expectations for them to move forward with the plan. For our part, we had to give people a reason to become a Cribs for Kids partner. Making this process simple and cost-effective was key to our success, but we also had to make enough money that we could stop spending our time and energy worrying about going broke. The price had to be lower than retail (with shipping costs included) while allowing us to build in extra for administrative costs. I felt $49.99 was the magic number. It fit our criteria and allowed us to say, "For fifty dollars you can save a baby's life." Unfortunately, Graco wanted to charge us $48.00. Making $2.00 on each unit was not going to keep our doors open. I was growing frustrated by our stalled negotiations. We couldn't walk away after coming this far, nor could we agree to an arrangement that didn't improve our financial situation. If we were going to front money for containers of Pack 'n Plays, we couldn't be operating on such slim margins.

Later that summer, on August 29, 2005, Hurricane Katrina made landfall in New Orleans. Like so many Americans, we spent the next few workdays glued to our computer screens watching in horror as the tragedy unfolded, feeling helpless to do anything. The morning of Wednesday, August 31, the *Pittsburgh Post-Gazette's* front page featured a picture from Getty Images of a mother in the Superdome sleeping on a cot cuddling her baby. I faxed it to Graco with a note that said, "This mother survived Hurricane Katrina, but her son could die in the shelter because he doesn't have a Pack 'n Play. What can we do?" Kory Pomon (who would eventually become our sales representative) got back to me immediately. He said, "We just had a meeting trying to figure out the best way to help. This is the answer!"

I got in touch with Judy Rainey. Thanks to her more than twenty-five years working in the Senate, she was able to connect with Louisiana Senator Mary Landrieu's office, which put us in contact with non-profits working on the ground in the Gulf region.

Within seventy-two hours a truckload of Pack 'n Plays, strollers, and swings were in New Orleans and distributed to shelters. Although it was a drop in the bucket considering the massive devastation in the Gulf region, we were grateful to have the chance to make a contribution. Cribs for Kids' experience in identifying and addressing areas of need and Graco's manufacturing and distribution power came together to make a difference. Working together so effectively from idea to completion on such a quick turnaround showed us that we were a powerful team, and our partnership could be greater than the sum of its parts.

Within a couple of weeks, we signed a deal making Cribs for Kids the nationwide distributor of our own Pack 'n Play model.

I am still and will always be a liberal Democrat, but I make no bones about the fact that Rick Santorum, a conservative Republican, is one of the earliest and most effective champions of Cribs for Kids. Without his vision and guidance, I don't know that we would have ever made the leap into crib distribution. I have tried to thank him for this, but he says, "Judy, I did nothing. If I told you how many people I've put in the office of presidents and

CEOs who couldn't close the deal…you closed the deal."
It's true that I have always had the passion to tell Cribs for
Kids' story in a way that excites people. The senator understood who needed to hear the story and got me in the
room, though. Even if I'd had the idea for a public-private
partnership on my own, it might have taken me years to
make the contacts. As Howard Heckes said, an introduction from a senator goes a long way.

There are many dangers inherent in our current
polarized state of politics. The most insidious is that
we've stopped seeing government officials outside our
party as representing us. *Not my president! I didn't vote
for him. Don't blame me; my side lost.* In the moment,
that might feel like blowing off steam, but if we think
that way for too long, we begin to believe it. I am a
lifelong resident of Pennsylvania, yet my first reaction to Joe James's suggestion that I approach Senator
Santorum was the fear that that might make me hypocritical. I had a cost-effective, noninvasive technique
for saving babies' lives to share with him, yet I worried
I might be booted from his offices if I were rooted out
as a liberal. Earlier in my career, I had sought funding from politicians on both sides of the aisle, under
Republican and Democratic administrations, and had
never thought twice about whom I had voted for. I was
their constituent, as were the people I was serving, and
that was all that mattered. How had I forgotten that?

When this *us vs. them* mind-set stops us from asking one another for help and sharing our ideas to improve our communities, we're in grave trouble. We have to be open to asking for help and to accepting it. Otherwise, we're holding everyone back.

Cribs for Kids Headquarters in Hazelwood on December 1, 2014.

The five ladies and their forklift—Eileen Carlins,
Barbara Clemons, Paulette Luczak, Heather Glaser,
and Judy Bannon (with author, Jennifer Bannon).

Ray Mansfield accepts a portrait from his Super
Bowl days with the Pittsburgh Steelers at the NFL
Alumni Banquet. Portrait by artist Tom Mosser.

Chuck Puskar, board chairman and founder of the Western
Pennsylvania Chapter of the National SIDS Foundation, takes
his turn roasting Ray Mansfield at an NFL Alumni Banquet.

Bob O'Connor volunteers at the Christmas
Gift Wrap booth at Century III Mall.

The magical billboard that disappeared and then
reappeared after a phone call from a friend.

The Pierogie Place, winners of the first annual
Pittsburgh's Perfect Pierogie Cook-Off fund raiser.

Meg Dougherty and Noreen Crowell have donated
twenty-four-hour answering services to us through
their company Meg-a-Phone since 1989.

District Attorney Stephen Zappala, Judy Bannon, Bob O'Connor,
and Gwen Elliott receive a check from Ronald McDonald House
Charities to help finance the first cribs distributed by SIDS of PA.

South Side Rotary Club, early supporters
of Cribs for Kids, in 1998.

District Attorney Stephen Zappala receives a donation
from District 3 of the Business and Professional Women's
Club members, Bernie Koval and Gwen Elliott.

Author, Jennifer Bannon, in our dorm-room
offices, in 1998, working on our first logo.

Board member Noreen Crowell and Judy Bannon, with actors
Zach Braff and Donald Faison, visiting the set of *Scrubs*.

Faison and Braff joke with Sean Crowell, Noreen's son and key grip on *Scrubs*. Sean coordinated the donation of a walk-on role on the long-running comedy show to Cribs for Kids.

Team Steps for Sammy, winner of the 2010 Breath of Life Stroll.

District Attorney Stephen Zappala, host of the annual
Women of Achievement Awards Dinners.

Dr. Michael Goodstein, medical director/researcher for Cribs
for Kids, in his model nursery at WellSpan York Hospital.

2012 Diamond Gala Honoree, Frank Coonelly,
Pittsburgh Pirates' president; his wife, Debbie; and host
Kevin Mullen at the Diamond Gala fund raiser.

Barbara Clemons, Judy Bannon, Tiffany Price, Heather
Glaser, Cindy Mols, Denise Puskaric, and John Robinson
stand with the first shipment of cribs to Saipan.

Pitt Ohio Express picking up a shipment
at Cribs for Kids Headquarters.

John Robinson and Denise Puskaric shipping
product from our warehouse in Hazelwood.

Board member Luci Casile, Chief Allegheny County Deputy
Sheriff Kevin Kraus, Allegheny County Sheriff William Mullen,
Pittsburgh City Councilman Cory O'Connor, Judy Bannon,
and Mike Manko of the district attorney's office tour our
warehouse at the Grand Opening of our new headquarters.

Eileen Carlins ready to give an educational
talk promoting safe sleep.

Judy Rainey at our booth at the 2015 AMCP
Conference in Washington, DC.

Annual fund raiser benefiting Cribs for Kids organized by the
Cruz and Phillips families in memory of David Angelo Cruz.

Our first shipment of *Sleep Baby Safe and Snug*
arrives from Charlie's Kids Foundation.

Judy Bannon with her family at the Ernst & Young
Entrepreneur of the Year Awards, summer 2015: Michael
James, Dick Bannon, Jennifer Bannon, Kelly James,
Judy, Jack James, Lacey Horvat, and Sean Bannon.

Lesson 6

● ● ●

CHANGE IS NECESSARY FOR GROWTH.

**Have faith that it is taking
you where you need to go.**

All great changes are preceded by chaos.

—*Deepak Chopra*

In the midst of working out the logistics of our new arrangement with Graco and drawing up contracts, an administrator from South Side hospital paid me a visit bearing bad news. University of Pittsburgh Medical Center (UPMC) had acquired the hospital in 1996 and had recently found a new use for our building, something we had been dreading for almost a decade. We would need to be out by March 2006, just four months away. Aside from recruiting new partners, devising a distribution system, and finding a warehouse, Eileen, Michaelleene, and I now needed to secure new office space and move before spring. I began to wonder if we'd taken on too much.

A few days later, I attended a committee meeting for our Daytona 500 fund raiser at the offices of the newly elected mayor of Pittsburgh and Cribs for Kids board chairman, Bob O'Connor. Bob, a rabid NASCAR fan, organized this fund raiser to introduce all of his friends to the joys of the first racing event of the year and at the same time raise funds for Cribs for Kids. An article that day in the *Pittsburgh Post-Gazette* explained that Bob was divesting himself from all the charities with whom he had been affiliated, with the exception of Cribs for Kids. (Our excitement at Bob's election was short-lived. Shortly after his inauguration, he began to experience headaches. Within a few months, he was diagnosed with lymphoma. He died nine months later at sixty-one. The city mourned the loss of their energetic, charismatic leader. I mourned the loss of my friend.)

At the end of the meeting as everyone was filing out, I said, "Bob, I have to talk to you. UPMC is ending our lease in March, and I still need to find a warehouse, cheap, ASAP because this partnership with Graco Children's Products is about to take off."

On the one hand, I was sure he had enough on his plate without having to hear about our latest problem. On the other hand, how do you not ask the mayor for help?

When Bob hesitated for a moment, an octogenarian sitting across the table from me said: "Honey, I have a warehouse on the North Shore if you'd like to use it." I looked up to see Art Schwotzer, chairman of Crossgates Inc., a real-estate development firm, gathering up his materials. What were the chances he would have warehouse space available and be the last person left in the room when I started this conversation? I didn't know Mr. Schwotzer, but I assumed that he had been invited by Bob. Later I found out that Bob thought I had invited him. It was like one of those holiday movies where the old man with the white hair and beard saves the day on Christmas Eve and then departs as jingle bells ring in the distance. We never did determine what brought this wonderful man into our lives, but we again chalked it up to the hand of God. I made an appointment to meet him at his warehouse the next day.

Mr. Schwotzer showed me around the warehouse himself. It was massive—thirty-five thousand square feet with four loading docks—and empty except for a few items in a dusty corner that were being rearranged by Mike Tarquinio, the sole tenant. An affable guy in his early forties, Mike ambled over to us and introduced himself right away, handing me a business card and engaging me in conversation about Cribs for Kids.

The building sat a block back from the banks of the Allegheny River across the water from the Strip District, just off of Interstate 279—easily accessible, yet tucked away in a quiet area that would allow plenty of room for trucks to pass in and out. It was a two-minute drive from downtown and fifteen minutes from our offices on the South Side. I was elated until I remembered that we'd never discussed price. With no desire to mislead Mr. Schwotzer and no time to pursue dead ends, I decided to go for brutal honesty.

"This is perfect, but I don't have any money to pay rent," I told him.

He smiled and then said, "That's OK. I brought the lease with me." He handed me a file folder. "It's one dollar a month. Can you afford that?"

As I lay in bed with my mind racing that night, I thought about how this warehouse could answer both of our housing issues. It was far bigger than we needed. Maybe we could take out a loan and build some offices within the space. Eileen, Michaelleene, and Jennie were all in the office the next day, so I asked them to take a trip to the warehouse with me. I wanted them to see the space, but I also wanted to float the idea of a build-out, to see if it seemed feasible in the light of day. When we arrived on site, I realized that the key I'd been given wouldn't fit the lock. Fortunately, I still had Mike Tarquinio's business card in my coat pocket. I dialed his number and heard a phone ring nearby. Looking around, I saw him in the parking lot across the street about to get in his car. "My key doesn't work," I half shouted, half spoke, unsure if I should talk to the phone or to him. He immediately ran over to us. When he walked up, he overheard Eileen and me discussing building offices in the warehouse.

"You don't have offices?" he asked. "I own that building next door. Come and see it."

A quick walk across the parking lot and we were inside a modern, three-story office building with a river view and a rooftop deck. A space had just opened up, and Mike thought it could be just right for us. While he discussed build-outs and parking, I tried to figure out how to tell him that whatever the rent was on this place, it was out of our league. I stayed tight-lipped, though, unsure if I was afraid to crush his dreams or my own. I thanked him for his time and told him I'd stay in touch. It ended up that I didn't have to. He was persistent in his pursuit of our business. Later that week, I decided to meet with him again to see if there was any chance of making this dream a reality. We were going to have to relocate somewhere. What could be better than having offices a stone's throw from our warehouse? As we talked, I learned that he'd received his MBA from Notre

Dame in 1990, the same day my son, Sean, graduated with his bachelor's. I began to relax. God had sent me a Domer. That had to be a good sign, right?

This delve into real estate was a big move for us, considering we'd been working rent-free for fifteen years. I called Senator Santorum's office and talked to Randy Vulakovich, the twentysomething staffer who had impressed me with his insightful questions at our first meeting. Not only was I seeking some business advice; the senator had just given us a check for $10,000 from his Good Neighbor Foundation, and I didn't want anyone in his office hearing through the grapevine that we were suddenly looking at posh riverfront digs. Plus, Randy was bright, and his position might carry some weight with Mike. He showed interest in seeing the building, so I invited him to pay a visit with me. Mike met us at the elevator and took us down the hall to look at the only spot that was available in the building. Not surprisingly, it dwarfed our current setup. (Plus, it was actually designed to be office space, not dorm rooms.) There was an entryway with room for a receptionist, a thirty-by-fifteen-foot room lined with shelves, and three twelve-by-twelve-foot rooms that would be perfect for individual offices. I felt spoiled just touring it, but Randy was not as impressed.

"Sorry, but this won't do. There's no conference room," he told Mike.

We'd never had a conference room. Hell, we didn't have a conference table. I wasn't sure if Randy was playing hardball or if he simply had great expectations for us.

"They can use this as their conference room," Mike answered, pointing into the large room with the shelving.

"No, that's going to be their workroom with their filing cabinets and office equipment," Randy said. "I'm not sure if you understand. This organization is going to grow incredibly fast over the next year. There will be dignitaries in and out of here all the time for meetings. A conference room is crucial."

What is this kid talking about? I thought. Conference rooms, workrooms, dignitaries? His list of demands was pretty long. Mine, on the other hand, was office space. Cheap. Now. I left discouraged and somewhat embarrassed, unsure if I was being an underachiever or a tease.

The next morning I was driving to work when Mike called. "Come to the building. I have something to show you."

Since our meeting twelve hours earlier, he had gotten together with one of his tenants, an architect named John Kudravy. The two of them had drawn up plans of a build-out they thought they could add to a second-floor space that was part of A & A Consultants, an engineering company who wanted to downsize their offices. The plans included three offices, a generously sized workroom, *and* a conference room.

"How will this do?" he asked.

Now I knew it. I was a tease. This man had gone so far as to enlist the help of an architect to accommodate our needs, and I'd never told him yet that we were broke.

"I'm afraid we don't have money for a build-out," I explained. "I know Randy's got high hopes for us..."

"That's OK. I like what you do, and it sounds like you've got a good business model. I'm willing to take a chance. We'll cover the build-out, and whatever you're paying in rent now is what I'll charge you per month."

I explained that our current space was free. He was silent for a beat.

"Well, I don't know if I can do that, but let's start you off at four hundred dollars per month. Can you afford that? You'll be honest with me. As your business grows, you can let me know, and I'll raise your rent." Who could say no to such faith and generosity?

Mike and his friend Joe Kappel, who also was a tenant, started to build our offices over the course of a few months while our time on the South Side ran out. Meanwhile, we continued to coordinate our first shipment of cribs with Graco. Because it would take ninety days for the initial container to reach us from China, they got us started with three hundred Pack 'n Plays shipped directly from their warehouse in California. In spite of the cavernous size of our warehouse, the sight of those three hundred Pack 'n Plays sitting within its echoey walls was overwhelming. All I could think was, *Oh my God, we'll never sell these before we have to pay for them.* More sleepless nights.

Our offices were finished on March 6, 2006, the same day I was being honored at Celebrate and Share's Women of Achievement breakfast for my work in the nonprofit sector. (Celebrate and Share is an organization created by Bonnie DiCarlo and JoAnn Forrester to raise funds for women and children in need and highlight the achievements of women in Western Pennsylvania. After the 2006 event, we teamed up with them to make this a fund-raising dinner that we host annually.) Between waking up at the crack of dawn to drive to the city in the dark to receive my award and coordinating with movers, utility companies, and computer technicians throughout the day, I was a nervous wreck. Luckily, my friend Cindy Mols (who eventually would come to work for us part-time after an early retirement) worked for Verizon and was able to facilitate a quick and smooth installation of our telephone services. While Jeff Klingelhoefer, our IT consultant, was hooking up our computers, the phone rang. It was a man named Steve calling from the Flint County, Michigan, Health Department.

"I need one hundred Pack 'n Plays, and Graco Children's Products told me that I had to call you," he said.

"Great, I can do that," I said. *OK, how hard can this be?* I thought. He needs cribs, and I've got them. To think I'd been worried about unloading them. Here's a third of them gone, right now!

"I'll need a shipping price before I can fill out my purchase order," he said. Sounded reasonable enough to me.

Oh, wait! I have to figure out how to ship these things.

I admit I thought I had some time to iron out that part because, well, it was going to take us forever to get these cribs sold, remember? Our customers were only going to need a couple at a time, right?

Luckily, it was almost five o'clock. "Is it OK if I get back to you in the morning? My shipping manager (*Who?*) is out of the office for the rest of the day." He consented.

It was another of those nights spent staring at the ceiling wondering how to make it over the latest hurdle. All I knew about shipping was FedEx, but I was pretty sure the guy who picked up our overnight envelopes stuffed with grant materials didn't have room in his truck for this delivery. The next day I was driving my new route to work, past the Pittsburgh Hilton and Gateway Towers along the Allegheny River. As I crossed the Ninth Street Bridge to our North Shore offices, a Pitt Ohio Express truck drove past me. *Oh, yeah, Pitt Ohio. I'll call them to get a price for shipping these cribs,* I thought. (This is Dick's favorite part of this story. "You had to ship cribs to Michigan, so you decided to call Pitt Ohio?" What he didn't realize was that it was the hand of God giving me another nudge.)

The first thing I did when I walked into the office was check my voice mails to see if the gentleman from Michigan had called back. Not yet, whew! Then I checked the Pack 'n Play box for its weight and measurements, happy that I knew at least that much about shipping, and looked up Pitt Ohio's phone number. Thankfully, a very patient salesman named Dave Decroo answered the phone. After giving him a little background on Cribs for Kids, I told him, "So I have one hundred Pack 'n Plays that I want to ship to Flint, Michigan. I need a shipping rate so my customer can fill out his PO."

"Great. Are they palletized?" Dave asked.

"I don't think I know what that means."

This is a moment when some people might have become exasperated, but Dave was patient. "Pallets are the wooden things you sit the boxes on so you can pick them up with a forklift," he explained.

"Oh. I don't think so." In actuality, I knew they weren't, but I tried to be vague in case this was a deal breaker.

"Do you have shrink wrap?" he asked.

"Well, no. But we can get some." I figured I would get Mike to help with that part if I could just get past this excruciating business of getting a price.

Not surprisingly, Dave could tell I had no idea what I was doing. He tried a different tack. "Do me a favor—write this up in an e-mail, including the part about what your organization is trying to accomplish, and send it to me by the end of the day."

Write an e-mail by the end of the day? Didn't he understand that Michigan had wanted a price yesterday? I needed his expertise, and he had yet to mock me or even speak to me in that slowed-down, deliberate way that car mechanics had been using on me since 1963, though. I could manage an e-mail.

The day's demands piled on top of one another in the way that can only happen when you're in the midst of moving offices across a city. Somehow I didn't manage to sit down to write Dave until late in the evening. That e-mail ended up being the bones of the grant proposals I would send for years, but at that time all I could think was, *Why won't he just give me the rates? Why do I have to go through all of this?*

First thing the next morning, I received a call from Dave. "I talked to the owner of Pitt Ohio, Chuck Hammel, and showed him your e-mail. He is so impressed with what you're doing that he said he would be happy to ship those for you." *Wait, had there been a possibility that they weren't going to ship them? This must be a competitive business.*

"Thank you. That's great…did you figure out a shipping rate?" I asked, trying not to sound as weary as I felt. *Why won't he just tell me the cost already?*

"Oh, no, no. You don't understand. Mr. Hammel is going to donate the shipping to you." I couldn't believe it. "That way, your customers can buy more cribs, right?"

"That's unbelievable! Thank you!"

"Before you get too excited, we're only in fourteen states," he said.

I hesitated for a moment. "Wait a minute, you mean it's not just this one time?" I almost felt presumptuous asking the question, but what else could he mean?

"No, we want to make this a regular service. What are you doing now?"

"Picking myself up off the floor."

He chuckled. "Can I come over and help you get this going?"

"Absolutely," I said.

Within two hours he pulled up to our offices in a Pitt Ohio truck just like the one that had inspired me to call him. He and Mike, our other savior, worked together to palletize and shrink-wrap our one hundred Pack 'n Plays while I called Steve in Michigan and told him there would be no charge for his shipping. He could not have been happier, and for the first time in a few months, I slept well. Life doesn't seem so intimidating with such goodwill in the world.

When I reflect on how Pitt Ohio has enabled us to thrive, I am awed. No question, the time and money they've contributed is staggering, but their impact goes beyond that. Their free-shipping donation was vital to our growth. Once word got out in the states they serve that you could put a baby in a Pack 'n Play for fifty dollars, shipping included, we were flooded with partner inquiries. They have always shown us the utmost care and respect, too. Having Dave Decroo step in to mentor me through the shipping process in those early days was a kindness that gave me confidence in myself and in Cribs for Kids' ability to succeed as a nationwide distributor of Pack 'n Plays. When you work for a nonprofit, you become used to a certain level of inconvenience that comes with donated services, knowing your needs will often take a backseat to those of paying customers whose business ultimately makes your donation possible. We have never experienced that with Pitt Ohio. When we call for a pickup, they show up as scheduled with a smile. In spite of all they have done for us, they have never sought recognition. It wasn't until 2013, seven years after I first contacted them, that Chuck Hammel consented to come to our national conference to receive our Starfish Award for his selfless actions, generosity, and motivation of others in making a difference in the lives of thousands of babies.

When we lost our space at South Side Hospital, I was overwhelmed. I suppose our offices weren't ideal, and they certainly weren't fancy, but they were home. The thought of leaving was disorienting, which it why it was also a blessing. Sometimes a shake-up is exactly what you need in order to grow. Like a plant that is limited by the size of its pot, our vision for how much we could grow was limited by those two rooms. That scary moment of looking into the future and not knowing where we would be forced us to envision something new. Trying to find a warehouse in close proximity to our offices had been a dead end; yet would we ever have considered moving if our lease hadn't ended? Once the offices were gone, we were free to find a warehouse anywhere and choose offices in its vicinity. (Believe me; it's much easier to find a few rooms of office space than a thirty-five-thousand-square-foot warehouse.) The warehouse led us to Mike Tarquinio and our new office building. Driving there, I saw the Pitt Ohio truck that led me to call them. It was their free shipping along with Graco's $49.99 price point that enabled us to entice so many new partners. That change that had seemed so insurmountable ended up positioning us for the growth we needed to move forward.

Lesson 7

● ● ●

A SMART LEADER SURROUNDS HERSELF WITH A STRONG TEAM.

Never doubt that a small group
of thoughtful, committed citizens
can change the world; indeed, it's
the only thing that ever has.

—*Margaret Mead*

"**M**y Barbara is leaving me!" I was on the phone with Betsy Hurst of Blair County Respiratory Disease Society, one of our first Cribs for Kids partners, who were located about ninety miles from Pittsburgh. I didn't have to ask who "her Barbara" was or why she sounded so panicked. Every time we'd spoken for the past year, Betsy had raved about Barbara Clemons, the dynamo who'd been helping run her Cribs for Kids program. Now Barbara was planning to move closer to Pittsburgh, and Betsy was beside herself.

"You have to meet with her! She's an incredible employee, she's brilliant, and she loves Cribs for Kids. You'd be crazy not to bring her on board," she told me.

We'd been in our new offices for a couple of months, and while our mission and workload had expanded, our bank account still hadn't. Hiring someone new seemed like the last thing we could afford. Every time we ordered a container of Pack 'n Plays (which was once every two months or so), we were taking a $57,000 leap of faith that we would be able to sell them. Even the sixty-day payment plan we'd negotiated with Graco didn't stop me from spending sleepless nights with my middle-of-the-night-panic brain imagining countless disaster scenarios. *What if we don't get more partners? What if we're left with a warehouse full of merchandise we can't pay for?*

Luckily, my light-of-day-business brain knew better. As it was, Eileen was immersed in education and grief support, Michaelleene was handling development, and I was busy with grant writing, lobbying, and recruiting new partners—all full-time jobs. When a Pack 'n Play order came in, we had to put aside everything else until it was taken care of, which had us steadily falling behind in our day-to-day duties. This whole model was based on the idea that our Pack 'n Play orders would increase dramatically, but how would we handle it if they did? I knew that we needed a better system and a staff member dedicated to distribution. I gave Betsy's Barbara a call and asked her to come in for an interview.

I knew the minute she began to talk that Barb was someone we needed in our office. Her knowledge of Cribs for Kids was vast—she already had a full under-standing of our vision and goals. Under Betsy's direc-tion, she had educated mothers and the community at large on the tenets of safe sleep, had demonstrated the proper setup and use of the Pack 'n Play, and had been on the partner side of placing orders for safe-sleep mate-rials through our office. Plus, Barb is African American, which put her in a unique position to appeal to our African-American mothers. The African-American cul-ture has a strong belief in bed-sharing, and we found that many mothers were reluctant to put their babies in Pack 'n Plays. As first-time moms typically look to their mothers and grandmothers for child-rearing advice, we were finding it difficult to persuade them to deviate from their generations-long practice of bed-sharing on the advice of a group of white women. Hearing this ad-vice from an African-American woman who had already raised her own son to manhood, a woman who identi-fied with the inclination to bed-share but still believed there was a better way, was much more effective than hearing it from someone outside the culture.

Prior to working at Blair County Respiratory, Barb had over a decade of experience in retail management. I knew that this meant she had a strong grasp of tracking inventory, working with suppliers, ordering merchandise, and, of course, managing people. Most importantly, I could tell that she possessed a never-ending supply of pure common sense, the most precious natural resource on the planet, in my opinion.

There was a wrinkle in this plan, however. At the end of the interview, she told me she wasn't moving to Pittsburgh but to Newcastle, about fifty miles from our offices. I knew that in our financial state, I couldn't pay her what she was worth. Add to that a long commute, and I didn't know if she would even consider accepting an offer. It's a testament to her belief in and commitment to the cause that she took the job at a lower wage with a daily travel allowance and a promise to be put on salary as soon as possible.

Barb started in May 2006, part-time. She often talks now about those first couple of months, when she sometimes spent her days rolling coins from donation canisters with a feeling of dread in her stomach that at any moment I would walk in and tell her we couldn't pay her anymore. Two nights a week, she took classes to become a Microsoft Certified Systems

Engineer at a local technical school, setting herself up with something more solid to fall back on. Every time she mentioned her classes, I felt a twinge of panic. I knew she wouldn't leave Cribs for Kids unless she felt there was no future in it. If we got to the point where she resigned, it would be a sign that we were in trouble.

She had become a vital part of the team, and I wasn't willing to lose her. Having her there to take on the ordering and shipping duties was a game changer for us. She designed a streamlined distribution process, standardizing and simplifying the ordering process for our partners and finding the best shipping rates for them. She was our liaison with Graco, coordinating container shipments and demand so that our partners would never have to wait more than a few days for delivery, while ensuring that we weren't struggling to pay for product that was sitting in the warehouse.

Before Barb joined us, there was always stress associated with Pack 'n Play orders. We never had the time to think through the process and become comfortable with it. Every big shipment was a mental and emotional drain. I think that our apprehension held us back. In the big picture, we were working toward the goal of distributing Pack 'n Plays nationwide, but on a daily basis, there was an element of "Oh no, we have too much work to do to deal with a big order today!"

Once Barb came along and took over the process so capably, we were ready, practically and physically, for orders to start rolling in.

Throughout the country, safe-sleep practices were catching on, and SIDS rates were dropping. Eileen and I were traveling constantly, visiting hospitals, health departments, and community groups; speaking at conferences; creating PSAs and videos; and spreading the word everywhere we could find an audience. With our new confidence in our ability to deliver the product, there was no stopping us. Every time we spoke, we converted new partners until we had gone from our original seven to thirty-two.

As popular as Cribs for Kids was becoming, we still found ourselves with financial worries. We needed to make more money to pay for administrative costs, but we didn't want to raise prices. After decades of having no idea how to reduce the risk of SIDS, we could now tell people that for fifty dollars they could provide a baby with a safe place to sleep, and donors were responding. Aside from the fact that fifty dollars is a bargain, it's also easy to calculate. One thousand dollars in grant money set aside? Twenty cribs. You have $10,000? Two hundred cribs. We were convinced that the ease of working with this price point was an ingredient in our success.

So if raising prices wasn't an option, where could costs be cut? We looked into the route the product was traveling to arrive in the United States. Graco covered the cost of bringing in the containers from China to Hesperia, California. From there we paid to have them shipped by rail to Pittsburgh at a price of more than $4,000 per container. That number had to shrink if we wanted to truly make a go of this. Barb and I initiated a conference call with our Graco representative, Kory Pomon, to see if they could either lower our per-unit price in consideration of the amount of product we were moving (that year we sold 4,100 units), or if there was an alternative shipping route. Kory worked out a plan to bring in the containers through the Panama Canal to the Port of Elizabeth in New Jersey, reducing our shipping cost to $700 per container. With this change in place, we were perfectly positioned to provide Pack 'n Plays to partners at an unbeatable price and still have enough money to cover the administrative costs of running our ever-evolving enterprise. By fall, we finally were able to bring Barb on full-time with the salary and benefits she deserved. We'd successfully thwarted the danger of losing her to the IT world.

That summer, Michaelleene announced that she would be taking an early retirement. She'd been at SIDS of PA nearly as long as I had, and we'd worked together in various jobs since the 1970s. It definitely felt like the end of an era.

In late November 2004, I had received a call from Dr. Lorraine Boyd, medical director of the Bureau of Maternal, Infant and Reproductive Health for the New York City Department of Health and Mental Hygiene (DOHMH). She had heard me speak at the American Public Health Association's conference in Washington, DC, where I'd announced the gratifying news that we had only lost four babies in Allegheny County at that point in the year, down from seventeen in 1998 when we first started Cribs for Kids. Dr. Boyd had been a believer in safe sleep even before the conference and was intrigued by our use of the Graco Pack 'n Play. She had tried her hand at giving full-sized cribs to mothers in need as we had at the beginning and ran into the same problems—their lack of portability and large size simply didn't work for the transient population and notoriously small apartments in New York City. After listening to my lecture, she believed that our program could be the answer. Now, in 2006, she was ready to seriously discuss becoming a partner.

"I need your pearls of wisdom," she told me over the phone. "All too often in this city, we see babies die in unsafe sleep environments just like you described. We have to implement your program. How do I become a Cribs for Kids partner?" Somewhere in the back of my mind, I could hear Sinatra singing. *If I can make it there, I'll make it anywhere…*

"It couldn't be simpler. I can send you the toolkit to-day. How many Pack 'n Plays do you anticipate ordering?"

"Probably about five thousand. Annually." Now my vagabond shoes were doing Rockette leg kicks under my desk. Five thousand Pack 'n Plays to one partner? That was more than what all of our existing partners had given out the whole year. There was a catch, though. Lorraine was sold on the program already, but she didn't have the final say.

"I need you to come to the city and teach my cohorts about Cribs for Kids, just like you presented it at the conference." Sinatra jokes aside, I knew that the impact of this partnership could not be overstated. This was one of the largest health departments in the country calling. We had to close this deal. In addition to Eileen Carlins, I asked Judy Rainey and Eileen Tyrala to present with me, bringing to the table their government and medical expertise, respectively. They both accepted, happy to be a part of this outreach to the largest metropolitan area in the country (and to spend a couple of days in the city). Lorraine set up a meeting with the DOHMH, Homeless Services, and the Administration for Children's Services (ACS), and we got to work preparing our presentation.

The two Eileens and the two Judys shared two hotel rooms in Little Italy, close to the DOHMH's offices so that we didn't have to do much navigating to get to our meeting. Their offices are across the street from

City Hall and its famous steps, which I recognized immediately as the scene of so many tense conversations on *Law and Order*.

In the morning we walked the few short blocks to the DOHMH, making our way up to the eighteenth floor with our Pack 'n Play in tow. Lorraine had filled the room with all the players she'd promised, as well as Nurse Family Partnership and various other professionals who worked with families and infants. We didn't have to do much to convince ACS. The department head fell in love with the Pack 'n Play as soon as he saw it. "This is exactly what we need for our babies! The mothers can work with this unit so easily," he told me. His enthusiasm helped us warm up the crowd, who became eager to learn more about our products, prices, and most importantly, our stunning drop in SIDS rates.

After the presentation, a large group of us headed to a Thai restaurant nearby for lunch. As we walked in, Lorraine said to me, "We may see Mayor Bloomberg here. This is his favorite restaurant." I played it cool, but the political junkie in me went on high alert. Even though he was not a member of my party, I had admired Bloomberg for years for his philanthropy, progressive views on women's issues, and stance on gun control. We were seated at a table long enough to accommodate our Cribs for Kids contingent, the Health Department commissioner, and Lorraine's staff. Sure enough, within a few minutes, there was a small commotion at the door. We looked up and saw plainclothes security guards enter (always betrayed by their clear earpieces and proclivity for talking into their sleeves). Then the mayor came through the door with Police Commissioner Ray Kelly. They had lunch together under the watchful eyes of the security detail—and the surreptitious glances of everyone else in the dining room. When I saw him get up to leave, I reached down into my purse and pulled out a business card. As he walked past our table, I stood up and said, "Mayor Bloomberg."

"Yes?" Conversation at our table stopped; forks clattered on plates. The looks on my lunch companions' faces said, *She did not just do that.*

"My name's Judy Bannon. I'm the executive director of Cribs for Kids, and I'm having a meeting with your maternal and child health workers. We're going to save babies' lives in your city."

"Oh, yes, I know what you do. Putting babies on their backs to sleep, right?" he asked.

"Yes, but we're taking it one step further. We're going to put them in safe sleeping environments. Every baby deserves a safe place to sleep." I handed him my card, and he took one out of his coat pocket for me. (You know that I still have it in my wallet, right?)

"Thank you for thinking about our babies. I will make sure this happens."

"Thank you, sir."

I sat back down and resumed eating my noodles.

"I can't believe you did that," Lorraine said.

"When I was sixteen, I shook John Kennedy's hand. After that, the rest is easy," I answered.

I wasn't naive enough to think that this brief encounter would put our cause at the top of his list, but I was glad that I'd spoken up nonetheless. Everyone at the table agreed that it couldn't hurt to be on the mayor's radar, even for a moment—and they figured that I was probably crazy enough to call him if things got dire. After lunch we walked back to the hotel, past the Health Department offices and the City Hall steps, where they were actually shooting an episode of *Law and Order*. Could this day get better? Not only would the New York City DOHMH be ordering Pack 'n Plays from us; so would ACS and Homeless Services, whose rep informed us he wanted safe-sleep environments for his shelters.

Our partnership with DOHMH was not only a financial boon; it inspired us to expand our line of safe-sleep products. One thing had been bothering me about the Pack 'n Play for a while—the sheets. Retail they were eleven dollars each, more than full-sized crib sheets. I was always afraid moms would buy those larger ones to save money and they wouldn't fit the mattress snugly, leaving the babies in danger of becoming entangled. When we negotiated the package with New York, Lorraine told me that she was interested in supplying Pack 'n Play sheets imprinted with the DOHMH logo to her moms, so Barb found a company online that sold imprinted sheets in bulk at a great price. I knew this was the moment to put my fears to rest and decided to print sheets with our logo and safety tips that we could sell inexpensively to all of our partners. Jennie was working for us part-time in those days. She has a graphic-design background, so I asked her to mock up a design.

"It should say that babies should sleep alone, on their backs. That no one should smoke around them... oh, and that there shouldn't be anything in the crib," I told her. I could tell she was wondering how we were going to fit all of this on a baby sheet.

"Do you want a list of tips? Should we just put the guidelines on it?" she asked.

"That might be too much. I think we want something simple, because they're not going to stop and read a ton of text while they're putting the baby down. Just something that sums it all up quickly, you know?"

After working on it for a while, she came to me with a design of the moon and stars with this poem underneath:

Now I lay me down to sleep,
Alone in my crib without a peep.
On my back in smoke free air,
Thank you for showing me that you care.

We've had that message on our sheets ever since.

Lorraine knew how to do things right. With each Pack 'n Play, she ordered two sheets and a Halo Sleep Sack to accompany them. Inspired by the way she'd fashioned a complete safe-sleep environment for her clients, we began to offer this package to all of our partners, calling it the Safe Sleep Survival Kit. Currently we also include pacifiers supplied by Philips, a Pittsburgh company that specializes in alleviating sleep and respiratory issues. The pacifiers they sell us are the same ones they supply to hospital maternity wards. We struck gold there, because we knew that if hospitals were using them, they'd already been safety-approved. Plus, they're slightly smaller than your typical pacifier because they're specifically made for newborns, and babies seem to have a special attachment to them. We get phone calls every week from mothers who are looking to replace that precious pacifier when one goes missing. They swear to us that it often saves the day when their little ones won't calm down for anything else.

Of course, our educational materials accompany every Pack 'n Play that goes out the door, too. Aside from safe-sleep checklists with working thermometers built into them so moms can ensure their nurseries are at an appropriate temperature, we include information on risks associated with cigarette smoke; literature aimed specifically at grandmothers; an infant safe-sleep video;

baby's first board book, *Sleep Baby Safe and Snug*; a picture magnet and brochures with our contact information; and a full-color photo of a safe-sleep environment.

Between designing and ordering the crib sheets and all the red tape involved in working with a government organization as mammoth as the DOHMH, we ran right up against their deadline. The first shipment had to be delivered by June 30, the end of their fiscal year. They couldn't pay for anything that wasn't in their possession by that date, so if there was any delay in shipping, we were out $30,000. The problem was that this deadline wasn't communicated to us until June 26. We were suddenly scrambling to get everything palletized and on the road. When I called the warehouse where the Pack 'n Plays were to be delivered, I found out that once the product was unloaded onto the loading dock, it had to be taken to the fifth floor of the building. This meant that the trucking company could not deliver them unless there was someone on the receiving end who could take them to their final destination. Of course, this was the weekend leading to Independence Day, so no one would be willing to commit to sticking around until the end of the day on Friday afternoon for the truck's arrival. Actually, there was one guy who agreed to do it—for a price. In the end I had to overnight a thousand-dollar check to a Teamster in Brooklyn to get the container emptied. Although I was

incredibly frustrated, it was a very *Sopranos* moment—
a shakedown of a charity, for God's sake. We were officially in business in New York City!

With me recruiting new partners, Eileen continuing
her education and bereavement work, and Barb running distribution, everything was on an upswing.
There seemed to be an energy carrying us forward,
drawing new opportunities our way. For example, at
the Women of Achievement breakfast where I'd been
honored a few months previously, Yvonne Cook, a
representative from the Highmark Foundation, approached me after my speech. She was impressed by
our program and told me about a grant her company
sponsored that she thought fit our mission. It paid
$220,000 over three years and could be used to finance
educational outreach. For years we'd struggled to find
grants that would pay for Pack 'n Plays. Now that we
were the Pack 'n Play distributors, we didn't have that
concern. There was no limit to how much education
we could provide, no fear that we'd whet the appetites
of mothers for whom we couldn't provide relief.

I had been writing grants for decades and had never
received anything near this amount of money, but I felt
that with Yvonne's belief in us, we had a strong chance.
For weeks we crafted our vision for how we would expand our education and gathered research data and

financial reports. As often happens, writing this grant was an invaluable exercise because it pushed us to articulate where we saw Cribs for Kids going and how we would get there. Happily, it ended up being more than an academic exercise. When we learned we had been awarded the money, there was dancing up and down the hallways of our offices. As thrilled as I was, though, I knew that three years goes by quickly. Our success distributing cribs was promising but not proven over time. When the grant ran out, we'd better be making enough money to compensate for losing that $70,000 per year. I knew that the missing piece to the puzzle since Michaelleene's exit was fund-raising. The time had come to hire a new director of development. Luckily, I knew someone who would be perfect for the job.

I had met Heather Glaser on Friday, February 3, 2006—two days before the Steelers were to win their fifth Super Bowl. The whole city was in party mode. Although we'd yet to move into our new digs, Mike Tarquinio had invited us to a Steelers party at the building so we could get to know our future neighbors. Heather, a vivacious woman who worked on the first floor for the Cystic Fibrosis Foundation, was there sporting her black and gold and circulating through the room. Initially, I thought she was asking so many questions about Cribs for Kids and trading nonprofit war stories to be friendly, but when she told me about her struggles as a young girl dealing with her mother's stillbirth, I could see that she had a more personal stake in our work. That experience had spurred her to make a career in the nonprofit world. I was intrigued by her. Her passion and commitment were evident not just in what she said but in how she spoke—emphatically, straightforward, brown eyes flashing. I asked her to tell me about some of the events she had planned for CF and was impressed by both the attention to detail and the money she had raised.

After we moved into the building, I kept in touch with her, talking as we bumped into each other in the ladies' room or on the elevator. In September, when she invited me to attend an upcoming event she had planned, the Wine Opener, I accepted, thinking this could be the perfect chance to see her in action. The event was held at the Sheraton Hotel and was attended by hundreds of guests. Throughout the evening I watched her coordinate wine, food, auctions, raffles, gift bags, DJs, hotel and CF staff, and volunteers. When I found out that event raised $60,000, I was convinced.

I invited her to lunch at Legends of the North Shore, an Italian restaurant close to our office building, to tell her more about Cribs for Kids and to gauge her interest in joining our team.

"Are you kidding? Why do you think I invited you to the Wine Opener? This was my plan the whole time!"

She accepted the job and came on board in January 2007, becoming the fourth member of our team.

Heather came to us with an event idea that she'd been kicking around in her head for years—an elegant holiday soiree featuring upscale jewelers displaying, selling, and raffling their wares. This became our Diamond Gala fund raiser, which we have held annually since 2008. In addition to the featured jewelers, the gala boasts top-shelf cocktails, a sumptuous dinner and desserts, music and dancing. At the Champagne and Diamonds table guests can buy a glass of champagne for fifty dollars (the price of one Pack 'n Play, naturally) that comes with a chance to win one of three diamond necklaces. Each year at this event we honor a local humanitarian who has made a positive impact on the city.

Doubling our staff reminded me once again that if you don't actively pursue growth, you'll stagnate. I've always believed in running a lean organization, never wanting to be one of those nonprofits that put more money into payroll than into their cause. I still believe that, but you also have to be realistic about your workload. Always keeping your head down and grinding away keeps you from seeing the possibilities around you. Our financial structure had changed drastically when we went from a fund-raising, grant-writing enterprise to a purveyor and distributor of products; yet we were still operating without a financial expert. I began to consider if we could afford to hire another employee.

In October 2005, our valued board member Jim Agras had invited me to a dinner where he was being honored. At the event when he accepted his award, he spoke briefly about his business, Triangle Tech, before saying, "The work I'm most proud of, however, is serving as a board member for Cribs for Kids." He proceeded to spend the rest of his time at the podium talking about us, even using his moment in the spotlight to ask me to stand and be recognized. His humble action was fortuitous. If he hadn't highlighted his work with us, I may not have reconnected with an acquaintance that was in attendance that night.

Between the dinner and dessert courses, a woman walked up to me and said, "Do you remember me?"

She looked familiar, but I couldn't place her.

"I'm Paulette Luczak's sister, Maryagnes." I had known Paulette in the nineties when she worked for an educational nonprofit called Pittsburgh Voyager that taught kids about math and science through hands-on lessons that took place on a former navy training vessel that was retrofitted for environmental education. For schoolchildren in the Pittsburgh area, no other field trip could compare to learning science while cruising on the city's three rivers. The classrooms were located on the vessel, but for a time, the business offices were across the hall from us on the South Side. Paulette had an education background, but when I knew her at Voyager, she was the office manager. I was always impressed by her analytical mind and skill with Excel and QuickBooks. Back then I was just learning that when you typed on a computer, the words appeared on a screen. Creating a spreadsheet in Excel was as foreign to me as writing a paper on a manual typewriter would be to a teenager today.

Maryagnes and I caught up on some personal details; then she told me that Paulette was still at Voyager and was looking for a new challenge.

"It sounds like Cribs for Kids is growing fast. Do you have any openings? You know, Paulette would be great on the educational or the financial side."

At the time I wasn't hiring anyone new, but I called Paulette to say hello. We reminisced, and she sent me her résumé to keep on file. When I read it, I learned that shortly after we'd lost touch, she'd been promoted to director of administration. Her duties included managing the internal financial processes of the organization; analyzing and communicating financial information to staff, board, auditors, government agencies, and private foundations; negotiating contracts; overseeing payroll; training employees in HR policies; researching and reviewing contracts, agreements, and other legal issues; and creating and implementing organizational policies and procedures for program scheduling. She was the only person I called when it was time to fill this new position.

When she came in to discuss the job, I knew that it was the hand of God who'd reconnected me with Maryagnes, and then Paulette. Not only did she have all the skills we were looking for, but she was an expert at things I didn't even know we needed until she mentioned them. Once again someone with the perfect combination of skills to help take Cribs for Kids to the next level had appeared out of nowhere. Paulette's background in teaching, nonprofit work, and administration was like a dream come true. In February 2007 she became our director of business operations.

Our team of five ladies was in place.

I have always taken great pride in being an independent woman with a sterling work ethic. Like many Americans, I used to think there was a kind of virtue in being overworked, believing foolishly that if you needed something done, you had to do it yourself. One of the most impactful lessons I have learned as the executive director of Cribs for Kids is that most of that philosophy is baloney. The sterling-work-ethic part holds up, but as our organization grew, I had to revise the rest of it. Smart leaders don't kill themselves working eighty-hour weeks until all of their drive and passion are sapped. They also don't try to be experts at everything. Smart leaders surround themselves with smart teams. Each time I considered hiring someone new, I worried that we couldn't afford it. The truth was that we couldn't afford not to. If we wanted Cribs for Kids' impact to grow, our staff had to grow beyond just Eileen and me. If you're smart about whom you add to your team, choosing those who bring positive energy, intelligence, and passion, they will add value beyond what you can count in dollars and cents. Not only did Barb, Paulette, and Heather all possess specific skill sets and expertise; they brought ideas for how we could educate more mothers, distribute more Pack 'n Plays, empower our partners more effectively, raise more money, increase our visibility in the community, and streamline our administrative processes. Just as importantly, they made our workplace a livelier, warmer place where each of us is supported in our work by the others.

The next time you find yourself drowning in work while you try to do it all, remember that the only prize you earn for being a workaholic is high blood pressure. Stop, take a deep breath, and look around. There's usually someone close by who is looking for a chance to shine. Be smart and let her.

Lesson 8

● ● ●

IF YOU WANT TO BE A TEACHER, YOU MUST BECOME A STUDENT.

*Education is not the filling of a
pail, but the lighting of a fire.*

—*William Butler Yeats*

In 2007 Cribs for Kids had thirty-two partners in sixteen states who were educating their communities about safe sleep and accessing local funding to fulfill our collective mission. Through our relationships with Graco and Pitt Ohio, we were able to provide them with Pack 'n Plays at the lowest price—even lower than Walmart—and quick, often free, shipping anywhere in the country. With all these elements and our team of five in place, we were able to let go of the fear that we wouldn't be able to provide for the mothers we educated. I knew that safe sleep was the next step to Back to Sleep, and I believed strongly that our new goal was to make our message as ubiquitous as Back to Sleep had been for over two decades. To do this, we devised a three-pronged approach that included: creating a collaborative environment where our partners could learn from each other and develop best practices that would strengthen our organization; enlisting hospitals to educate new mothers; and, bringing together safe-sleep leaders to create a comprehensive curriculum to roll out to the professional community.

If we wanted to take Cribs for Kids to the next level, we first needed to empower our partners. Having learned many lessons throughout my career about the value of tapping into the talent surrounding me, I knew that our people were our greatest asset. Our intention in structuring the organization as a partnership rather than a hierarchy had been so we could more quickly and effectively spread safe sleep throughout the country. There was a hitch, though. While we had relationships with our partners, they didn't have relationships with each other. There was no partner identity or camaraderie, no established best practices, and no opportunities for them to learn from or lean on each other. That lack of interaction was limiting our potential.

Our monthly online newsletter and website message board weren't dynamic enough to create a community. We had to provide a forum for meaningful, authentic interactions if we wanted to harness the power of our whole organization. When I thought about the large network of personal and professional allies I had made throughout my career, I realized that I had met most of them at conferences. I discussed this with my team, and they agreed that hosting a National Cribs for Kids conference in Pittsburgh was the solution.

We called the conference "Breaking the Cycle—a Safe Sleep Summit." Our stated goals were starting a national dialogue about safe sleep and the accurate and consistent classification and coding of sudden, unexplained infant deaths; inspiring a grassroots movement to push for legislation to standardize infant death-scene investigations and reviews according to CDC protocols; and bringing together Cribs for Kids partners to share best practices. We invited partners, public-health professionals, doctors, first responders, and top researchers such as Dr. Rachel Moon, Dr. Fern Hauck, Dr. James Kemp, Teri Covington, and Dr. Carrie Shapiro-Mendoza, as well as Thomas Hargrove and Lee Bowman, two Scripps Howard reporters who had researched and written a seven-month-long investigative series entitled *Saving Babies: Exposing Sudden Infant Death in America*, which addressed the need for standardization in the way sudden, unexpected infant deaths are investigated and classified. (Through this series of articles and a push by coroners throughout the country, the term SUID—sudden, unexpected infant death—began taking prominence over the term SIDS. SUID includes SIDS deaths and deaths from suffocation and rollover, which are preventable.)

In preparation, Heather and I took meetings with hotel managers and catering directors and worked on the two-hundred-page conference syllabus. Eileen and I planned the agenda and worked with the state to offer continuing-education credits (CEUs) to attendees. Barb handled the logistics, creating displays and giveaways and figuring out how to transport everything from our offices to the hotel and back again. Paulette coordinated registration and continually ran the numbers to keep us within our budget. We chose to hold the conference at the Omni William Penn, the storied hotel where I'd met JFK as a girl. Its location in the midst of Downtown Pittsburgh with a variety of bars, restaurants, and common gathering areas on its premises and in the surrounding area would give attendees plenty of space to socialize. We planned a welcome reception with Pittsburgh-inspired hors d'oeuvres and an open bar, purchased a block of tickets for a Saturday-night Pirates baseball game, and stocked the hospitality suite with snacks and drinks. Our hope was that we'd hit the perfect balance between professional and personal networking opportunities to begin building a dialogue and community.

Upon arriving on the seventeenth floor of the hotel, the area where all the action was to take place, attendees were given a tote bag (actually a high-end diaper bag donated by Graco) filled with items about the city and the conference. Since this was before the days when most people were accessing information easily from their smartphones and iPads, we loaded them down with a conference syllabus in a three-inch binder containing speakers' biographies and printouts of their PowerPoint presentations. We wanted to make sure that everyone left the conference equipped to educate their communities.

With so many partners coming together for the first time, the Welcome Reception felt a bit like the first freshman dance of the year. In the room were those who'd been in the SIDS community for a long time; they were the popular kids whom the others had heard about and admired from afar. Then there were insulated cliques of friends and colleagues who stuck together because they didn't know anyone else, and the occasional wallflowers who had traveled to the conference alone, usually from our smaller partners who couldn't afford to send more representatives. Of course, everyone was cordial, but the feeling was somewhat tentative as people introduced themselves and made small talk for the first time.

Over the course of three days, we learned from each other, shared meals, and cheered our way through a very soggy Pirates game. As I walked through the hotel, I'd see new friendships forming over drinks and laughter in the lobby and notice increased conversations in the corridors between sessions. Q&As became livelier as everyone got more comfortable sharing their thoughts with the group.

We ended the conference Sunday morning with a session called "Where Do We Go from Here?" Before calling the room to order, I stood at the podium for a moment and looked around. What a difference a few days had made. New friends sat in clusters chatting as if they'd known each other for years; ideas brewed among those with like-minded concerns; business cards and hugs were exchanged before everyone headed home. After some thank-yous and preliminary remarks, I began the conversation by asking the participants if they felt the conference had been worthwhile. I was answered with applause and affirmations.

"You've had a few days to meet and share your ideas and strategies, your hopes and challenges. Where do you think Cribs for Kids should go from here? What is our future?" I asked.

Hands shot up around the room beginning a lively discussion that would last for over an hour. One of the key ideas that came from that discussion was the decision to enhance our Cribs for Kids Toolkit with documents and tips contributed by our partners. Today the toolkit contains over one hundred documents partners have eagerly shared with their counterparts throughout the country. Once again, many hands— and hearts and minds—had lightened the load.

"So, should we have another conference in a couple of years?" I asked. But I already knew the answer. Since 2008 we have had a national conference every two years (with the exception of our third, which was held in 2013 so as not to conflict with the International Conference on Stillbirth, SIDS, and Infant Survival that was held in Baltimore in 2012). Each year we have more attendees than the last. Those three days act as a catalyst for the new ideas that keep us moving forward and help us to grow our Cribs for Kids community, our most treasured resource.

When we first began Cribs for Kids, our only contact with the mothers we served had come through the request letters they wrote to us. Once we became the distributors, local moms came to our offices whenever possible to pick up their Pack 'n Plays. This gave us the opportunity to educate them face-to-face. When they arrived, Barb or Eileen would walk them through a training that included watching a brief video about infant safe sleep. (Eileen Tyrala was the executive producer of the video, *Safe Sleep for Your Baby Right from the Start*, which was produced by Cathy Melfi through a grant from the Innovator Circle Grant Program at Abington Hospital.) They then answered a questionnaire about sleeping and living conditions in their homes. We had a Pack 'n Play set up in the room with a babydoll in a Sleep Sack lying in it so they could see exactly what their safe-sleep environment should look like. We were ostensibly the educators in the scenario, but we were learning invaluable information about the needs and concerns of the mothers as we talked to them and answered their questions. We loved the personal touch that this experience provided and found ourselves wishing more of our clients could receive face-to-face education. We knew that the amount we could offer in our offices was limited by space and time constraints, so we asked ourselves, "Who regularly comes into contact with new mothers and would be qualified to provide this sort of training?" Nurses, of course.

In 2002, Pennsylvania had passed a law requiring hospitals to furnish mothers with educational materials about Shaken Baby Syndrome before discharging them. We began to consider similar legislation insuring that new mothers be taught about safe sleep and given a Pack 'n Play if they needed one. If this happened before they even took their newborns home, there would be no reason why their babies should ever lack a safe place to sleep. Through training moms in this practice, nurses would become experts in safe sleep, which would most likely lead them to practice it in the hospital nurseries and encourage moms to do the same. We would also be assured we were reaching every woman who gives birth in a Pennsylvania hospital.

In early 2005 I received a phone call from Pennsylvania State Representative Michael Diven. His mother, a nurse at Allegheny General Hospital in Pittsburgh, had heard me speak about safe sleep at grand rounds there. Excited about the possibility that safe-sleep education could eliminate many of the infant deaths she had seen over the years, she had urged her son to contact me. Michael proposed an amendment to an existing crib-safety bill that would mandate safe-sleep education in the commonwealth's birthing hospitals. The amendment was introduced on April 13, 2005, but did not pass.

In 2007, when we decided to focus our attention more fully on education, we knew the time was ripe to pursue safe-sleep legislation again. Eileen Tyrala approached her neighbor Larry Curry, a member of the Pennsylvania House of Representatives and longtime supporter of children's issues, about writing a free-standing SIDS-education bill. In February of 2008, he introduced House Bill 1752. In March, the Health and Welfare Committee held a hearing where Eileen Tyrala, Eileen Carlins, and a couple from Philadelphia whose baby had died of overlay all testified to the importance of this education. The bill came out of committee and passed the House of Representatives in October of that year. However, in the Pennsylvania state legislature, bills have to be passed by both the House and Senate, or General Assembly, before the end of a two-year period. That period expired before we were able to get the bill through the Senate, in part because of pushback from the Hospital Association of Pennsylvania, who actively lobbied against it because they believed it was asking too much of hospitals and nurses who were already weighed down with many responsibilities.

We were committed to this idea, however, and decided that we had to prove it would work. Eileen Tyrala and I set up a meeting with Pittsburgh's renowned Magee-Women's Hospital of UPMC. It is Pennsylvania's largest birthing hospital—eleven thousand babies are born there each year, about 45 percent of births in Allegheny County. We began by explaining the statistics—that SIDS and SUID are the number-one causes of infant mortality after one month of age and how many babies were dying each year—and then introduced Cribs for Kids and safe sleep. After we showed them how we'd impacted Allegheny County's SUID rates over the past ten years, we explained our vision for how they could be a part of that success. Our plan was to provide them a short instructional video (the same one we used in our in-office training) that their nurses would show to each new mother before she was discharged. The nurses would simply put the video on in the room and explain to the mother that she must pay attention because afterward she would be required to sign a form asking if she had seen and understood the video, if she agreed to put her baby in a safe-sleep environment, and if her baby had a safe place to sleep. Cribs for Kids would provide Pack 'n Plays and sheets to the hospital free of charge so that if a baby did not have a safe sleeping place (or if the mother had a bassinet, which is only safe for the first few months of life), the hospital social worker would be alerted to bring a Pack 'n Play and sheet to the mother before she went home.

Honestly, I thought this would be a no-brainer since we were offering a lifesaving intervention that wouldn't cost the hospital anything. However, at the end of the meeting, they thanked us for our time and told us they weren't interested in taking part. They actually did cite the reason everyone had predicted—that nurses were already too busy.

"The nurses are overworked. Plus, they have to train and educate the mothers in a variety of areas, including teaching them how to bathe their babies," we were told. (Mike Goodstein was incredulous about this reasoning, "Unfortunately, as a neonatologist I have had to pronounce many babies dead, and none of them have ever died from having dirt behind their ears!") Even our argument that the nurses would not actually have to teach but merely turn on the video and hand over the commitment form did not change their minds. As they began to thank us for coming, I took one final crack at it.

"I understand that it seems like a tall order. My concern is this. Now you've been taught about these statistics and have been offered a program at no cost that will help save babies' lives. We're even offering free Pack 'n Plays and sheets to your patients. If you don't do this, and babies born at Magee continue to die because their mothers didn't know about safe sleep or didn't have a safe-sleep environment, well…"

At 10:00 the next morning, I got a call from them. "We gave it some thought, and we think we'll do that program after all."

Once we had Magee on board, we asked St. Clair Hospital, which averages about fourteen hundred live births per year, to be the other participant in the pilot program. That way, we could tell the legislators, "It doesn't matter how large or small the maternity ward; this program will work there."

The program was so successful that soon we had the other four birthing hospitals in the county interested in participating. They all wanted what Magee—their most celebrated competitor—had. We also began working with two managed-care organizations (MCOs), Gateway Health Plan and UPMC for You, to motivate mothers to attend their prenatal visits. Low-income mothers often miss these visits because it is more difficult for them to find transportation or to take time from work because they don't have paid time off. Skipping these medical appointments can have a negative impact on an infant's health, however. We were able to convince these MCOs that offering moms Pack 'n Plays as a reward for attending all their prenatal visits is a great incentive. Currently we have eleven MCOs participating. These days many mothers have safe sleep environments, so they are given the choice of a stroller, high chair, or car seat. All of these incentives come with infant safe-sleep materials, including a Halo Sleep Sack and the educational materials that are included in our safe-sleep survival kit.

After a year of running our hospital initiative, we began lobbying for a SIDS-education bill again, armed with multiple sources of data that showed that our pilot program in Allegheny County was a success. At the suggestion of Randy Vulakovich, who was now our government-affairs advocate, we sought out a champion in the state Senate. That champion was John Pippy, a senator from Western Pennsylvania, whose friends had lost their son in an unsafe-sleep environment while he was at childcare. This experience had made Senator Pippy newly passionate about spreading safe-sleep education. In January of 2009, Larry Curry and Pippy simultaneously introduced companion bills, House Bill 47 and Senate Bill 577. For the next two years, we all worked tirelessly getting the bills in and out of committees, but even with these bipartisan efforts, we still struggled. Late in the game, we learned that the Pennsylvania Hospital Association was still actively lobbying against us.

In September 2010, Jim Agras came to our rescue again. The bill was sitting on the desk of Joe Scarnati, Republican and president pro tempore of the Senate and Jim's good friend. After Jim spoke to him about the importance of the bill and the positive impact it would have on the infant mortality rates in the commonwealth, Scarnati put his power behind getting it passed. The day of the Senate vote, Eileen, Barb, Heather, Paulette, and I clustered around my computer while Eileen Tyrala sat at her computer in Jenkintown to watch the session live on PA C-Span. It was grueling, after all the work we'd done, to know all we could do at this point was bite our nails, pace, and wait. The tension was ratcheted higher when a senator who had indicated he would support the bill voted nay. In the end, five years after we began our quest to make infant safe-sleep education mandatory in Pennsylvania's hospitals and birthing centers, we triumphed. Act 73 of 2010 was signed into law by Governor Edward Rendell on October 19, 2010. Since then, we have provided the bill language to our partners, which, to date, has helped get similar laws passed in half a dozen other states.

Once we had a permanent presence in the state's hospitals, Mike Goodstein saw an opportunity to incentivize them to become more willing and engaged advocates. His years of experience as one of WellSpan York Hospital's attending neonatologists put him in the perfect position to create a program that would enhance the work hospitals do rather than overwhelm them. He spearheaded this effort, implementing various practices while documenting the work through data collection, presentations, and finally the publication of his article "Improving Infant Sleep Safety through a Comprehensive Hospital-Based Program" in the journal *Clinical Pediatrics*. This work eventually turned into the National Safe Sleep Hospital Certification Program, which today sets out clear guidelines for hospitals to follow to achieve three levels of Safe Sleep Certification status. To achieve the bronze level, or Certified Safe Sleep Hospital, institutions must develop a safe-sleep policy statement that incorporates the AAP's Infant Safe Sleep Guidelines, train staff on the policy, guidelines and the modeling of safe-sleep practices, and educate parents to practice safe sleep. To become a Certified Safe Sleep Leader at the silver level, hospitals must also replace the receiving blankets in their nurseries and NICUs with wearable blankets like the Halo Sleep

Sack and audit and report their progress to Cribs for Kids. Hospitals that attain the gold level, or Certified Safe Sleep Champions, take the extra steps of affiliating with a local Cribs for Kids partner or becoming a partner themselves and provide a safe-sleep environment to at-risk parents in their communities. (As of this writing, thirty-three hospitals across the country have qualified to be certified through this program.)

Another opportunity to educate the professional community came when the Pennsylvania Department of Health (PADOH) put out an RFP looking for a group to provide safe-sleep education throughout the commonwealth. We had not had much luck receiving funding from them previously, but our work in the Allegheny County hospitals helped us secure this grant. In addition to educating childcare providers; providing bereavement support; and collaborating with the Pennsylvania Chapter of the American Academy of Pediatrics, Pennsylvania Child Death Review, the Chiefs of Police Association, and the division of Children Youth and Families, the cornerstone of the grant was our Infant Safe Sleep Symposia, which brought together a team of experts to provide full-day trainings in each of the six health districts in the commonwealth.

A variety of professionals such as nurses, social workers, EMTs, and coroners attend these trainings. A typical symposium starts with Eileen Tyrala sharing her impeccably researched "History of SIDS" presentation (upon which the "Brief History of SIDS" chapter in this book is based). Mike Goodstein then discusses the definitions of SIDS and SUID and the necessity of diagnosing each properly so that accurate data is recorded for research purposes, as well as the genesis and effects of the AAP's change in sleep-position recommendations. After lunch Mike introduces our hospital initiative, and Eileen Carlins talks about bereavement services for grieving parents. Chuck Kiessling, coroner of Lycoming County, and Vick Zittle, program director of the Pennsylvania Child Death Review Team, explain how to perform proper death-scene investigations. Photographs of actual death scenes are used to help demonstrate and explain unsafe sleep environments and categorize them according to risk. I close out the day talking about the work we do at Cribs for Kids and how to become a partner.

Because some mothers continue to resist safe sleep, we focus special attention on overcoming barriers to successful implementation, including dispelling the misconceptions that bed-sharing is not a risky practice and that safe sleep is antibreastfeeding and antibonding. To limit resistance of medical staff, we address their concerns about time constraints for parental education and assuage their fears that back sleeping could lead babies to aspirate if they vomit in that position.

The first Safe Sleep Symposium took place in 2010 in Lancaster, Pennsylvania. We are now on our second contract with the PADOH and continue to hold the trainings in hospitals and birthing centers throughout the state.

The Pennsylvania and Florida Chapters of the AAP have a program called EPIC (Educating Practitioners in the Community.) Eileen Tyrala approached Susan Yunghans, Executive Director of the PA AAP, with the idea that infant safe sleep would be the perfect subject for an EPIC program. In 2013, with funding from the PA AAP, the CJ Foundation, and Cribs for Kids, she developed the program "Decreasing Preventable Deaths in Infants: Spreading the Safe Sleep Message" as another outreach to the medical community. Knowing that even the busiest of us have to eat, she sets up lunchtime training sessions at doctors' offices, hospitals and public health organizations, bringing the staff their noon meal and safe sleep education, literally exchanging food for thought.

Deb Robinson, a SUID investigator from Washington State, created the Cops 'n Cribs program which enlists public-safety officers in the fight for infant survival. A former marine and sheriff's deputy, her involvement in the SIDS Foundation of Washington began after her son, Ian, died in 1991. Throughout her career she became convinced that law enforcement could play a crucial role in connecting mothers to public-health services. Cops 'n Cribs trains officers, who are frequently in private homes as they answer distress calls, in the tenets of safe sleep and provides them with Pack 'n Plays to distribute. The officers are empowered to start conversations with families of infants about where the baby sleeps and judge if the sleep environment in the home is safe. Each patrol car carries a Pack 'n Play in the trunk, which officers can gift to the family on the spot, along with safe-sleep education. Not only does this program ensure babies in their communities are safe; it helps build strong, positive relationships between police and the citizens they protect. We were so impressed by this innovative avenue of education that we asked Deb if we could partner with her. In 2013 we hired her as the director of public-safety initiatives at Cribs for Kids to take this program nationwide.

In spite of the positive impact safe sleep has made, not everyone is a believer. In fact, various groups have come out against it. Lactation consultants believe there are safe ways to bed-share and encourage this practice as a way to enable tired mothers to breastfeed more easily in the night with less interrupted sleep. (We are strong advocates of breastfeeding—as long as mothers feed their infants while sitting upright. Our belief is that there is no safe way to bed-share.) Attachment-parenting followers believe that bed-sharing promotes a stronger bond between mothers and infants and helps both feel more secure in the night. (We advocate room sharing, keeping the baby's crib next to the parents' bed, not bed-sharing.) Some bed-sharing advocates, such as Drs. James McKenna and William Sears, actually believe that babies of breastfeeding mothers are safer sharing a bed with a parent, rather than sleeping in a crib, because their parents are in close proximity to attend to their nighttime needs.

With differing messages circulating, we decided that it would be beneficial to parents to establish a consistent safe-sleep message. In the spring of 2011, Judy Rainey invited a small group of people working in the area of safe sleep to her family vacation home in Bethany Beach, Delaware, for a weekend retreat to discuss how to tackle this challenge. The group included Teri Covington, Deb Robinson, and me. It was then that we created the Coalition Against Unsafe Sleep Environments (CAUSE) to forge a partnership of the private, nonprofit, consumer, and government sectors working on the issue of infant safe sleep. The coalition capitalizes on the broad array of knowledge and experience we all bring from the injury prevention, SIDS, child welfare, and maternal and child health arenas to create a simple yet powerful campaign that warns parents against the dangers of bed-sharing and other unsafe sleep environments.

In her capacity as our director of national and legislative affairs, Judy invited organizations to join

CAUSE. Presently we have twenty-nine organizations involved throughout the country. A presence on Facebook and Twitter and an infant safe-sleep listserv provide information, resources, and a discussion platform for many like-minded organizations. Before her retirement from the Senate Judy had worked with Senator Frank Lautenberg on the Stillbirth and SUID Prevention, Education, and Awareness Act of 2009. He and Representative Frank Pallone from New Jersey introduced the bill in the US Senate and House, respectively, in July of that year. If the bill becomes law, it will improve SUID investigations, data collection, services, and prevention. One major component of the act is the expansion of the "Back to Sleep" campaign to include all infant safe-sleep recommendations.

Our Safe Sleep Ambassadors program is another method we use for disseminating our message to the general public. The program is based on the African-American proverb "Each one teach one." To keep slaves subservient in the American South, they were denied education. However, some slaves learned to read and write in secret and considered it their duty to teach another slave. As we travel throughout the country educating nurses, first responders, medical staff, and other infant advocates, we encourage them to share what they learn with friends and family so that our message continues to travel once we have returned home. After our trainings, we hand out certificates and buttons that say, "I'm a Safe Sleep Ambassador" and impress upon them that it is now their duty to teach what they learned to three other people. (Our Each One Teach One philosophy has been adopted by the NICHD who subsequently introduced their Safe Sleep Champions modeled after our Ambassador program.)

When we got our first batch of buttons, I put one on my denim jacket and forgot about it. A few days later, I left for the international SIDS conference in Australia. As I was ordering my breakfast at Au Bon Pain in the Pittsburgh International Airport, the woman behind the counter saw it and asked me what a Safe Sleep Ambassador was. We got to talking, and she told me that her daughter had just had a baby. She had heard of safe sleep but wasn't sure what it was.

"Well, don't they say the baby can sleep on his side, too?" she asked.

"Actually, back sleep is recommended," I answered, and I related the rest of the guidelines to her (making myself popular with the travelers waiting in line behind me, I'm sure), ending by handing her my card so she could revisit the information on our website. *Well, I guess that's one person I've taught. Two more to go*, I thought to myself.

While I was going through the security line, the TSA officer asked me to remove my button before going through the metal detector.

"What's a Safe Sleep Ambassador, anyway?" he asked. *Ah, my second student has appeared.*

I told him, and we ended up in a similar conversation to the one I had earlier. (Again, I was making friends all over the airport, holding up lines like I was.)

I met up with Teri Covington, executive director of the National Center for Child Death Review and my good friend, at LAX; we were on the same flight to Sydney.

"What's that?" she asked when she saw the button. I could tell by her tone that she thought it was a little silly, like the Duran Duran buttons my daughters adorned their jean jackets with back in the '80s. I told her all about the SSA program. "You can't believe the people who will ask you about this! Just today I've already had two conversations about safe sleep with people who knew nothing about it. Imagine when nurses wear these in maternity wards and NICUs. There will be countless teachable moments when moms ask, 'What's a Safe Sleep Ambassador?'"

She still seemed a bit uncertain, probably attributing all these conversations I'd had to my tendency to chat with strangers unbidden. However, as we were waiting in line at customs, a man in front us said, "Safe Sleep? Is that when you put babies on their backs?"

"Well, that's part of it," I answered. Teri and I found ourselves in a ten-minute conversation about safe sleep, our work, and the conference.

When we were done talking and the man turned back around, Teri said, "All right, give me one of those buttons." She wore it throughout the whole trip.

As had always been the trend, our focus on education led to an increased demand for Pack 'n Plays. Barb, our one-woman distribution center, was becoming severely overworked. We needed a labor force, but hiring more employees was going to put us right back on the ropes with our finances. As had always been the case, most of our volunteers were senior citizens looking for a way to stay busy in retirement. This work was much too physical for them. Joe James, my daughter's father-in-law who'd set me up with Senator Santorum's team, gave me another great tip. He told me about Renewal Inc., a private, nonprofit organization "dedicated to the renewal of individuals in the criminal justice system and to their return to society as responsible citizens." To fulfill this mission of providing reentry and rehabilitation services for ex-offenders, they are always looking for nonprofit partners for whom their residents can perform community service. They house many people in their twenties and thirties, just what we needed for this labor-intensive job.

Barb called their offices and arranged for a crew of four or five volunteers to come to the office for a trial run. We had a container of Pack 'n Plays arriving and hoped they would be able to help us through what was always a crushing all-day experience. Five men arrived ready to work. Barb briefed them on what needed to be done, and they jumped right in. What usually took us eight hours was finished in less than three. All the men were professional and courteous, never complaining. When the work was done, we ordered pizzas and soda for everyone and all sat down to lunch, starting the process of getting to know each other.

That was the first day of what has turned out to be a long and fruitful relationship between Cribs for Kids and Renewal Inc. For the past eight years, we have had their volunteers at our offices daily. When inventory is light, the crew cleans the warehouse and helps with other projects like assembling safe-sleep survival kits. On our busiest days with Pack 'n Plays heading back out the door as quickly as we unload them from the truck, they never stop moving until it's time for our now-traditional pizza lunch at the end of the shift.

Barb always takes the time to explain our mission and how the work in the warehouse helps us fulfill it. There's power in realizing that each crib you process could save a baby's life or at least will give that baby a warm, clean place to lay down her head. Most people who volunteer with us return again and again, knowing that they are making a difference. We've learned that there's an unwritten oath at Renewal that when one of our guys is released, he personally finds someone to replace him on our crew so we're never at a loss for good workers.

With the problem of physical labor solved, we decided to hire someone to come in two or three days per week to help with orders and invoicing. Luckily, I had the perfect person in mind. Cindy Mols, a friend I'd met at my McKeesport Business and Professional Women's Club meetings, had recently taken early retirement from Verizon and was looking for something to keep her busy a couple of days a week. Her efficiency, intelligence, and delightful personality were a perfect fit.

Everything was running great for a while, but then a new wrinkle appeared. As we knew would happen eventually, Art Schwotzer sold the warehouse. It was time to find a new place to store our products. Luckily, Mike Tarquinio had a warehouse in McKees Rocks, about six miles from our offices, and offered us space there. His place was smaller than Art's, and he used it for his own storage, so the amount of inventory we could keep there was limited. We found ourselves in a constant balancing act for a while, trying to keep enough inventory to fill orders within a reasonable time frame without running out of space to store it all.

To alleviate the situation, we rented two fifty-three-foot trailers that we parked in the back lot of our building. Our board member Gary Mangan built wooden docks that pushed up against the trailers right under the doors. Barb had just enough room inside the trailers to stack and shrink-wrap one pallet. When the trucks came to pick up, she'd use a pallet jack to lift the pallet and roll it out the door onto the dock and into the truck. The whole process worked in reverse when trucks were dropping off. Each trailer was secured with a padlock. The first day we came to work in subzero conditions, we found out the padlocks had frozen. Barb made cozies for the locks so they wouldn't freeze again. It was far from ideal, but it was our reality.

It went on this way for months until one day Mike Tarquinio called me to say, "Your wish has come true." I knew right away what he was going to tell me—the tenants who rented the garage in our office building were moving out. The garage was fifteen hundred square feet, big enough to act as a warehouse, and was adjacent to nine hundred square feet of office space. We were finally going to be able to get rid of our trailers and move all our inventory into the building. The only hitch was that the garage didn't have a loading dock, so we would have to buy a forklift.

I called Dave Decroo at Pitt Ohio to see if he could recommend a place where we could buy one at a good price. "Let me look into it and call you tomorrow," he said. I should have known his MO by then, but I didn't suspect a thing.

Sure enough, the next day when he called back, he said, "Mr. Hammill would like to donate a forklift to you." Now, I've never said no to a donation before, but this was too much, right?

"Oh, I wasn't asking for a donation. I just thought you might be able to recommend someone who sells them."

"Don't be silly. Now, it's not a new one, but if you ever have any problems with it, we'll pick it up, repair it, and bring it back to you. Also, we'll supply the propane and do regular maintenance on it."

My husband calls it the Most Embarrassed Forklift in America because we spray-painted it pink, blue, and white in keeping with the color scheme of our logo. Adding to its uniqueness is the shrink-wrap roof the Renewal crew constructed for it one day when they had some downtime so that Barb won't get wet when she unloads containers in the rain.

Not surprisingly, Pitt Ohio has remained true to their promise to upkeep our forklift. The one day it broke down, they sent over a flatbed truck to collect it within hours. Mind you, this shipping company had to rent that truck because none of the trucks in their fleet have flatbeds, but they never blinked an eye. When they arrived to pick it up, they had a replacement forklift for us to use during the couple of days it would take them to repair ours and return it.

From the beginning, we said that the goal of Cribs for Kids was to be more than a crib giveaway program. We knew that having a Pack 'n Play wouldn't lead a parent to always lay down her baby safely anymore than having a refrigerator full of veggies leads us to always eat well. What we didn't know then is that education is not an end in itself. It is a continual process. When you're young, your goal is to prove how much you know. As you grow older, however, you become aware of how much you don't know. This realization sets you on the path to wisdom, leading you to more questions and opening yourself up to new knowledge.

At the beginning of our journey, we stumbled upon a piece of knowledge—many babies diagnosed as SIDS were dying in unsafe sleep environments—and felt compelled to teach others that many of these deaths could be prevented. We felt such an urgency to spread this message that we almost went broke in the process. Paradoxically, this outreach was ultimately what saved us. As we taught more people, we lit the fire in them to teach others and to seek their own knowledge. Their investigations led them to discoveries that they added to ours until safe sleep grew into not just one idea but an entire body of knowledge and practices. While we may have been the experts at the beginning of this journey, we are now just as often students—learning from our partners' and colleagues' experiences, from scientists' safe-sleep research, from bereaved parents' stories of loss, from first responders' and medical examiners' death-scene reports, and from doctors' and nurses' frontline experiences training new mothers.

In 2007 when we set the goal of educating the world about safe sleep, we had thirty-two partners in sixteen states. By 2010 we had grown to 250 partners in forty-six states. We didn't accomplish this incredible growth by being teachers; we did it by being members of a community of learners. In Lesson 2, we discussed the importance of realizing you may be the expert you seek. That's a valid lesson, but it is a beginner's lesson in nerve and self-esteem that is meant to get you on your way. As you travel farther on your path, you must be willing to accept and embrace that you will always be a student. True wisdom begins when you realize how much you don't know.

Lesson 9

●　●　●

KNOW YOUR MESSAGE AND
SHARE IT WITH THE WORLD.

*Listen to your own voice, your own
soul, too many people listen to the noise
of the world, instead of themselves.*

—*Leon Brown*

At the beginning of this journey, we were pioneers.
Now we live in a world where safe sleep is discussed
everywhere from the AAP to mommy blogs, from state
health departments to Facebook. If you had told us in
1998 that by 2015 there would be widespread discussion of safe sleep throughout the country, we would

have thought that meant we'd reached our goal. What we didn't count on is that getting your message out to the public is not the type of goal that can ever be completed, especially in this era of social media. In our early days, educational materials consisted of printed trifold brochures that we sent through the mail and handed out at events. If we were lucky, we'd occasionally get a PSA played on the radio or TV. If we wanted you to get to know us better, we'd put you on our mailing list and send you our printed quarterly newsletter. These days, without a website and a strong social-media presence, you might as well not exist.

One of the most confounding modern experiences is the almost total inability many of us feel to distinguish truth in a sea of "expert" information. It used to be that if you wanted to learn more about something, you would go to a library or bookstore and find a few reputable sources to read, or you would turn to the newspaper or Peter Jennings to explain it to you, and that would pretty much be it. These days there are so many avenues of information—websites of varying degrees of validity, advice from nonexperts on social media and blogs, and twenty-four-hour news stations competing to be first with the news, even if all they're reporting is speculation. It feels impossible sometimes to know what is true, because every issue has not just two sides but multiple sides with multiple people battling to convince you that their take on the situation is the right one. How did it get so complicated to learn facts?

As an organization with a lifesaving message to communicate, we have had to find ways to set ourselves above the fray. In professional circles we have established a solid reputation through years of successful implementation of our program. To mothers who have never heard of us, though, it's not enough to provide factually correct information and advice. We also have to be the top search result on Google that links to a professional, comprehensive website. That website alone won't be enough to reach our audience, though; we must also have a presence on Twitter and Facebook. And of course none of this matters if the information isn't presented in a way that helps moms feel confident that what they're learning from us can be trusted.

Heather is in charge of our media communications. A part of her job that once consisted mainly of writing press releases has expanded over time to include all new media platforms. Although effectively communicating and marketing through these methods requires a whole new set of strategies, she has always had an innate understanding and appreciation for how they work. When I first hired her in 2007, our website was very basic. A forward-thinking board member, Mark Davic, designed it as a labor of love in memory of his daughter, Madeline. At that time we didn't realize the

FIVE LADIES AND A FORKLIFT

importance of this innovative form of communication. Keeping it updated was always the last thing on our minds. Because of that, we put very little money into it and had scant understanding of how it worked. It took us hours to make even minor updates because we didn't invest in the most current software.

Heather had bigger ideas for what our website could be, but I was skeptical. She built her case, telling me about her visions for message boards and FAQs for partners and new moms, an online toolkit, and educational resources that could be accessed by anyone with the Internet (which was increasingly becoming everyone). However, none of this could happen using the site we currently had. Eventually she convinced me that we needed a whole new site. She found a local company who would give us a nonprofit discount and began taking meetings with them. Over six months she created all the content, approved every image, proofed countless pages, and spent days going back and forth with the designers over things that seemed minor to me, like making sure the colors of the on-screen logos were true to our printed version, but are ultimately what communicate our professionalism to users. Of course, none of these things matter if your website isn't functional. If a user becomes frustrated because he or she can't find what they seek or pages are slow to load, she will go straight back to her Google search and choose the next result. Heather spent hours surfing through our site before it went live to ensure that users would have a positive experience.

Today our website is integral to the work we do. Mothers in need of cribs can find contact information for their local partners. Those seeking advice can refer to it for up-to-date information on safe-sleep research and guidelines. They have expert guidance at the click of a mouse through our "Ask the Pediatrician" feature, which allows them to ask Eileen Tyrala any questions they have about their infants. (An added bonus of this is the comprehensive FAQ we have created from their correspondences. It also keeps us in touch with the questions that are on moms' minds.) Our Partners section provides all the tools needed to run a successful Cribs for Kids chapter—no more sending binders through the mail. Recently we created an e-commerce store where partners can get quotes, order their supplies, and track shipments. All of our educational materials are housed online too, along with information on bereavement support, fund-raising events, and past and upcoming conferences. Our About Us section, which includes our history and staff bios, and our Media section, which catalogues our appearances in print, radio, and TV, help establish the credibility that users want to see when seeking advice from an online source. What I once thought of as a necessary evil has become an indispensable tool for fulfilling our mission. Heather also controls our social-media presence through our Facebook and Twitter accounts, which drive traffic to the website and enable us to post new research studies, SIDS rates, and reminders to keep babies safe.

Disseminating the facts isn't enough, though. Sometimes we have to actively counter misinformation. One example that has had us working overtime is creating a new image of how a crib should be decorated—or not decorated. It's a cliché, but a picture truly is worth a thousand words. For decades a cigarette dangling from the mouth of a movie star was the ultimate image of cool. About fifteen years ago, a comprehensive campaign was launched to reduce cigarette smoking in the United States. In conjunction with a series of chilling public-service announcements, positive images of cigarette smokers virtually disappeared from mainstream media, while real-life smokers were forced to cower in the streets as they indulged in this unhealthy habit. Kids today have so little interest in smoking that catching them lighting up is barely on parents' radar screens. When this generation sees someone smoking, they think "cancer," not "cool."

Images of babies sleeping in piles of fabric and pillows are the new Marlboro man. So many people still picture a crib filled with stuffed animals and fluffy blankets as the ideal sleep setting that when they see a baby in a Sleep Sack lying on a fitted sheet in an otherwise empty crib, it doesn't make sense to them. If that image of safe sleep became the norm, though, mothers would begin modifying their infants' sleep environments without even thinking about it. Overstuffed cribs would go from "darling" to "dangerous" in their minds, without any direct education taking place at all.

In September 2009 Dr. Rachel Moon and Brandi Joyner of the Children's National Medical Center published a study in *Pediatrics* titled "Infant Sleep Environments Depicted in Magazines Targeted to Women of Childbearing Age." The study found that 36 percent of images in these magazines showed babies in unsafe sleep positions, while 64 percent showed them in unsafe sleep environments. Knowing the impact of visual imagery, we found these statistics alarming, to say the least. We knew how irresponsible the images were, but we understood that the people creating the ads and photo spreads most likely did not. Mike Goodstein saw this as an educational opportunity with the potential to have nationwide impact. In 2010 he put together an online petition aimed at making advertisers aware of this danger and imploring them to use more responsible sleep images in their campaigns. Cribs for Kids helped draw attention to the petition by sharing it with our partners and other contacts. Over sixteen hundred individuals signed, along with letters of support from several major SIDS organizations including Cribs for Kids, the CJ Foundation,

Safe Kids USA, First Candle, and the American SIDS Institute. Mike sent the petition to Bob Linden, who was senior vice president in training and development at the American Association of Advertising Agencies (4A's.) Bob hooked him up with his colleague Portia Badham, VP of marketing. Earlier in her career, Portia had worked at Children's National Medical Center and was thrilled to get back to her roots in child advocacy. For six months Mike, Rachel, and Portia worked on collecting sample images, perfecting the wording of the guidelines, and determining how to disseminate the information into the advertising community. 4A's pushed out the information to over 750 agencies.

Throughout this process, they have found that the lack of safe-sleep imagery in stock photography is making it difficult for magazines and advertisers to affordably follow our recommendations. Through discussing the problem with partners, we learned that Sam and Maura Hanke and Kate Menninger Desmond of Charlie's Kids Foundation, another nonprofit focused on promoting safe sleep, were also concerned with this issue. We are currently working with them to find professional photographers who are willing to provide pictures for a repository of safe-sleep images that will be free to advertisers and anyone else eager to model infant safe sleep in the media.

While it's true that you can buy a laptop at Target these days for $300 to $400, the price of high-speed Internet can be prohibitive. As Netflix and similar services gain popularity, cable companies have had to shift their cost structures to lower cable prices while increasing Internet costs. Luckily, in the age of the smartphone, you can access online content without Wi-Fi. For many low-income families, smartphones are the most reliable and affordable way to get online. Realizing this, we had to consider how friendly our website is to those users. Navigating through an extensive website can be difficult on a small screen, which is why apps were invented. Unfortunately, when Heather looked into the cost of creating an app, we were told it could run us anywhere from $30,000 to $70,000.

Dr. Christopher Conti joined our board around that time. Aside from being an emergency-medicine physician, he is also senior pastor at Emmanuel Baptist Church in Rankin, a borough about eight miles from Pittsburgh.

"Judy, I've been thinking that you need an app. The young people in my church use their phones for everything. If they could access your safe-sleep information without having to navigate through the website, it could make a real difference," he told me.

"I agree. We've been talking about the same thing. I just don't know that we can afford it right now. We're still looking at the numbers."

"Well, my church got an app through a company called Subsplash. They create apps free of charge for ministries. I believe that what you do is a ministry. You're doing the Lord's work, right? Let me tell them about your mission and see if they'll help you."

I was grateful for his assistance, but I wasn't sure if Subsplash would see it the same way he did. To my surprise and delight, they agreed to fund an app for us. (We paid them less than $1,000 for its creation and pay a modest monthly fee to maintain it.) Once again Heather put on her techie hat, working with them day and night for weeks until it was perfect. Because of their generosity, we are able to offer the app for free, something that we would probably not have been able to do had we paid to have it created. To me the beauty of the app is not just that it can be accessed with the touch of a finger, but that every time a mom surfs around on her smartphone, she sees the icon. Even if she doesn't open it, that visual reminder keeps safe sleep in her mind.

Dr. Conti gave us another gift when he introduced us to Brittany Johnson, a young woman in his congregation. She was looking for part-time work while she studied for her MCATs. Obviously, he knew all too well the stress and commitment involved with that. When he and his wife were going to medical school, they were blessed to encounter many people who offered helping hands along the way. He wanted to give back by helping Brittany, so he asked if we had any open positions. Honestly, we didn't, but I trusted his judgment and was so grateful for what he'd done for us that I invited her in for an interview. As soon as we met her, we knew she would be an asset. Her kind heart and passion for serving others were clear from the start. We hired her to job share with Cindy and help to plan our third national conference.

One of the first events Brittany attended was the 2013 Women of Achievement dinner. That year one of our honorees was Maggie Hardy Magerko, president and owner of 84 Lumber, a company that was started in Eighty Four, Pennsylvania, by her father, Joe, in 1956. I was eager to find Ms. Hardy Magerko at the cocktail hour that night so that I could share my personal connection to her family business. Their headquarters was a few miles away from where I grew up. My sister Diane's job fresh out of high school was working as Mr. Hardy's very first secretary. Their main form of advertising was a monthly flyer that listed sale items and specials. Help was needed to get these mailings out, so I was hired to work in the mail room. That was my first job, and I loved it. I still remember the smell of the freshly cut lumber mixed with the ink from the Gestetner machine that printed the labels. (Social media is not accompanied by such wonderful aromas.) Maggie was touched by the story, which harkened back to a time when she was just a little girl.

Later, while I was at the podium sharing the story of Cribs for Kids, I noticed someone from her table approaching our table and conferring with Heather. I was trying to stay focused, but I could see a small buzz was building among my staff, and I couldn't help but feel anxiety. As I finished my talk, I was approached by Dennis Noonan, VP of sales and marketing for Nemacolin Woodlands Resort, which is also owned by the Hardy family. He asked if he could say a few words. I handed over the microphone to him, not knowing what was coming. "Maggie Hardy was so taken with your story that she would like to make a one-hundred-thousand-dollar donation to Cribs for Kids," he announced to the room. My mouth dropped in amazement. He then invited Maggie to say a few words. She reluctantly came to the stage and spoke about how our conversation had gotten her reflecting on the early days of her company and the struggles her father went through as a small-business owner. Listening to our story, she saw parallels between it and 84's, from humble beginnings in Pittsburgh to nationwide expansion.

I had been wanting to start a matching mini-grant program for our partners but didn't have the funding until that moment. Her donation became the Joseph A. Hardy Sr. Mini-Grant Program, which offered $2,500 grants to forty partners who could prove they were able to match the grant with donations from their local communities. Our hope was those donors would become regular supporters. The grantees, who were selected from hundreds of applicants, have become some of our most successful partners. This experience with Ms. Hardy Magerko showed me that, even in these days of social media, sometimes a simple message, spoken from the heart, is still the most effective.

It's fascinating to think about how communication has changed in such a short time from direct mail newsletters and educational brochures to websites, social media, and apps. However, the most important lesson about communication isn't in how you say it but in what you say. Other people can teach you *how* to communicate, but if you don't have a powerful message to impart, ultimately no one will hear you. For years we struggled to figure out how to get the best price on cribs, how to distribute them, how to get others to join us, and how to pay for all of it. That's just about every question you think you would need to have figured out if you wanted to make Cribs for Kids a success, right? In spite of how long it took us to answer all of those questions, we continued to grow by leaps and bounds, often faster than we could manage. How is that possible? It's because we had a powerful message, and we shared it with the world. Everywhere we went, we told our story with passion, and people responded.

Yes, it's important to tweet and post and update, but it's more important to have something to say. Think about why you do what you do and what has gotten you to where you are, why it matters to you, and why other people should care. Then go out into the world and tell your story to anyone who will listen. Be excited and informed. Be vulnerable and bright-eyed. Be vocal and be you. The world will respond.

Lesson 10

●   ●   ●

GIVE YOURSELF CREDIT FOR YOUR ACCOMPLISHMENTS, EVEN IF THEY FEEL SMALL TO YOU IN COMPARISON TO YOUR GOALS.

*The key to realizing a dream is to focus
not on success but on significance—
and then even the small steps and
little victories along your path
will take on greater meaning.*

—*Oprah Winfrey*

In July of 2014, I was featured in a series called "People Making a Difference" on 90.5 WESA, one of Pittsburgh's public radio stations. Diane Beckstead, a music teacher at St. Luke's Lutheran School, happened to be listening and was inspired. In spite of the temperature reading on her dash telling her it was eighty-seven degrees, her mind was on Christmas, specifically the holiday musical she was planning to write for her students that year. At St. Luke's the kids don't perform the traditional Christmas pageant. Instead, Diane writes original musicals that focus on and benefit worthy causes. Because theater requires an exploration of emotions, she believes these musicals have the power to engage her students, as well as their audience, on a deeper, more empathic level than when they learn about the same issues only through news stories. The students also have the gratifying experience of bringing an important message into their community. She hopes this will inspire them to take active roles in solving societal problems throughout their lives.

Diane's ears perked up when she heard me talk about Cribs for Kids. Naturally, the audiences at elementary-school performances are filled with parents of young children, so she began to think about the impact safe-sleep education could have on them. She called me a few days later to ask how I would feel about her writing a Cribs for Kids musical. As you know by now, I have had plenty of dreams and visions for our organization throughout the years, but a musical was beyond what even I could imagine! I was instantly intrigued and gave my blessing.

Six months later my staff and I traveled to St. Luke's for the afternoon matinee of *No Crib for a Bed*, the story of a little girl cast as Mary in her school's Christmas pageant who causes a fuss when she refuses to put the baby Jesus down to sleep in a bed of straw. Having lost a younger brother to unsafe sleep, she knows the dangers. The solution? A Pack 'n Play, of course, which sits center stage holding baby Jesus at the end of the show.

Not only was the musical touching; it was beautifully written and performed. Diane and her students impressed us so much we couldn't stop talking about it for weeks. We wished that everyone involved in Cribs for Kids could see it. We were in the midst of planning our fourth national conference, which we figured would be the ideal venue for a repeat performance. Thankfully, we had an intern, Andrea Wilson from Carlow University, who had taken on the monumental task of acquiring all of the documentation from keynote speakers and presenters that was necessary to offer CEU credits to our attendees. With that piece handled, we were able to work with Diane to add the musical to the agenda.

The conference, Completing the Circle—Infant Safe Sleep and Injury Prevention from Data to Action, was held in April 2015. On the last full day of festivities, Diane loaded up 150 elementary students in school buses with all of their props and equipment and traveled an hour into Downtown Pittsburgh to perform on a makeshift stage in the Grand Ballroom of the Omni William Penn Hotel.

In the play, the baby who passed away is named Charlie. Diane chose that name after I shared with her the children's book *Sleep Baby Safe and Snug*, written by pediatrician and best-selling author Dr. John Hutton for Charlie's Kids Foundation, which was founded in honor of Sam and Maura Hanke's son Charlie who died in an unsafe sleep environment. Diane was touched by the book and asked if I thought they would be open to her naming the baby in the musical after him. After talking to Diane, they agreed. That Christmas she sent them a copy of the lyrics and music of the song "I'm Told I Had a Brother." They were in the audience that day at the conference and were overwhelmed with emotion to hear the song performed live.

"I can't even express how much it meant to Sam and I to see that in person. We don't have milestones with Charlie like we have with our other kids, no first steps or first word. We will mourn the lack of a first-day-of-kindergarten picture this fall. However, we have other 'moments' with him. The first time this occurred to us was in Tennessee when we announced that every baby in the state would be getting our book. We felt like proud parents. Seeing *No Crib for a Bed* was one of those momentous days. I sobbed through the whole thing, but it is an experience I will hold in my heart always," Maura told me later.

The Hankes lost Charlie on April 28, 2010. Sam is a pediatric cardiologist; Maura was a kindergarten teacher. They were devastated that a lack of education had led to their son's death. With their backgrounds, they couldn't believe that they didn't know the safe-sleep guidelines. *If it can happen to us, it can happen to anyone*, they realized. They knew that they had to teach other parents. In 2011 they established Charlie's Kids, a foundation dedicated to spreading the safe-sleep message to other parents. The primary educational tool they use is *Sleep Baby Safe and Snug*, baby's first board book, which tells the story of a mother preparing her baby for bedtime. Teaching safe sleep through a children's book is ingenious because it reminds parents of the safety guidelines while reading to their children at bedtime, exactly when that information needs to be top of mind. Also, while pamphlets and brochures often get tossed out, most people recoil at the idea of throwing away books. The book is education that will remain in the home.

After the performance we invited about one hundred of the conference attendees—mostly partners and presenters—to our offices for dinner. As we dined together, we marveled at the students' talent and had to laugh at ourselves thinking of how shocked they must have been by the buckets of tears we wept as they sang and danced, figuring that they couldn't have understood just how deeply connected we all were to the subject matter.

The reason we had this celebration at our offices instead of at the hotel was that a few months before the conference, we had moved again, and wanted to show off our new space. In April 2014, when the highest-priority item on our to-do list the week of our board meeting wasn't running financial reports but trying to figure out where to put the Pack 'n Plays that had overtaken our conference room, we had to admit we had grown out of our North Shore offices. It wasn't just the office space that was cramped; there was no room in our warehouse, either. We had three containers of Pack 'n Plays (more than forty-five hundred units) stored offsite at US Cargo, a division of Pitt Ohio Express, and two more containers in a warehouse in New Jersey. Keeping less inventory in stock wasn't an option for a couple of reasons. One, it takes ninety days for us to get Pack 'n Plays into the country after we place an order with Graco. Leaving a baby without a Pack 'n Play for any length of time because our stock is depleted is unacceptable to us. Also, we often send supplies as part of relief efforts during natural disasters. When Hurricane Sandy hit the East Coast in 2012, New York City requested two thousand Pack 'n Plays right away. If we hadn't had them on hand, they would have had to make requests to multiple suppliers and probably would have still come up short. That was a wake-up call, telling us we always needed to keep excess inventory somewhere in the States. All of this shuffling of product around the country was turning into a logistical nightmare, however.

Heather suggested we meet with Bridget Gaussa at Oxford Development, a commercial real-estate provider and developer based in Pittsburgh. Bridget's brother had died of SIDS some thirty years before, and, along with her sister Molly (who is one of our board members), she has been volunteering for us since the early 1990s. Within a week Jeff Deitrick, a senior vice president at Oxford, paid us a visit to discuss leasing a new space.

Emily Carlins, Eileen's daughter, who had graduated from the University of Pittsburgh School of Social Work with a master's degree, was working with us part time while searching for a job in her preferred field of geriatrics. A few days after our meeting with Jeff, she came into my office. "I was driving down Second Avenue through Hazelwood on my way in this morning, and I saw a building with a sign that said 'Office and Warehouse Space for Lease.' I wrote down the phone number."

I wasn't sure how I felt about Hazelwood, which had been an area in decline for the past few decades, but Emily explained that it was right across the Glenwood Bridge, making it easily accessible to those of us who lived south of the city and in close proximity to Downtown. I decided to take the number and called a few times, but I never heard back. I was about to give up, when Barb, always the voice of reason, suggested we drive over to check it out.

The site—easily accessible, large parking lot, well manicured—was promising enough to encourage snooping. When we peeked in the windows, we saw a man inside. I motioned to him to come to the door. He was one of the owners and was more than happy to take us on a tour. Barb and I played it cool, only allowing our faces to light up when his back was turned. We knew right away that this spot was ideal. The warehouse was fifteen thousand square feet—ten times the space we had at River Avenue. The office space was about sixty-five hundred square feet, three times what we were used to. Of course, there were some potential glitches. For instance, the owner stated that if we wanted to rent the warehouse, we needed to take the open-plan office space on the first floor which connected to it, not the second-floor space which was designed more to our liking. I wasn't sure I wanted to put money into a build-out. Still, I couldn't stop thinking about the building that whole weekend. I had a gut feeling that it was our next home.

I called Jeff first thing Monday morning to see if he could handle the lease for us. I also told him that the owner had told us the cost per square foot would be "triple net." I had nodded my head in understanding when he'd said that, but in truth I didn't know what triple net meant. Jeff informed me it meant that we'd pay the cost per square foot as well as the taxes, the insurance on the building, and maintenance costs. When he gave us an estimate of the rent, my spirits deflated. It was too much money no matter how I tried to rationalize it. Paying taxes didn't sit well with me either, since as a nonprofit, we're tax exempt. If we didn't pay the taxes, though, the owner would have to, and why would he agree to that? That was when I realized we couldn't lease the building; we had to buy it. I did the math again, amortizing what I figured the building was worth and how much of that we'd have to finance, and finally arrived at a figure I liked. The mortgage payment would be about 50 percent lower than the monthly lease price. I called Jeff.

"I want that building, but I don't want to lease it. I want to buy."

"They're only interested in leasing. Buying isn't an option," he told me. I knew that the world hadn't changed *that* much since I'd sold houses for Ryan Homes back in the 1970s. Everything's for sale if you find the right price. I asked Jeff to put together a contract that included two offers—one to buy, one to lease—just to see what the response would be.

He presented the contract to the sellers on Thursday morning, May 1. That evening I had a meeting after work, my card club of more than thirty years. When I arrived home, Dick said, "I taped the six o'clock news for you. You'd better watch it."

"There are rats the size of cats walking the streets of Hazelwood!" claimed an irate woman at the top of the hour. "They're all coming from the recycling plant off of Second Avenue," she continued. I recognized the building she was standing in front of. It was the one I had just offered to buy, and the recycling plant she mentioned was right behind it.

"What are you going to do now? Did you already make the offer?" Dick asked.

"This is the best news ever! Now they're definitely going to sell!" I told him, as if it were the most obvious conclusion.

The next day I called Corey O'Connor, Bob's son and Hazelwood's city councilman. I told him about our interest in the building and said, "You have to do something about those rats."

"Believe me; we're already on it. The city has invested millions of dollars into Hazelwood. They *will* get rid of the rats." That Saturday night I was at a fund raiser at the Hollywood Theater, a nonprofit movie house that mostly shows classic films. The mayor of Pittsburgh, Bill Peduto, was attending, too. He explained that the rat infestation happened because the recycling plant had shut down after the company went bankrupt and abandoned the building. The city was investigating the safest method for disposing of the vermin.

"We can't poison them because of the eagle's nest," he explained. For the first time in decades, Pittsburgh was home to a family of bald eagles who had nested not far from our building, and the Internet was captivated by the livestream video chronicling their activities. Obviously, nobody wanted to watch them dine on poisoned rats. The situation seemed a little more complicated than I'd anticipated, but I kept the faith. After all, we're talking about a plague of rats. Sounds like the hand of God to me.

On Monday Jeff called to say, "You're not going to believe this. They're going for option number one! They want to sell the building."

"I guess they heard about the rats as big as cats," I said. Later that day, the news came out that a new company had accepted the bid to take over the recycling plant. The rats were gone within weeks.

After a few days of offers and counteroffers, it was official: we were going to be property owners.

Luci Casile, treasurer of Cribs for Kids' board, is a vice president at PNC Bank, so I e-mailed her to talk about a loan. She suggested we set up a meeting at our offices so her boss could learn about Cribs for Kids' history, see our distribution center, and review our financials. She called me a few days later to say that if we put 20 percent down, she could give me a rate of 3.65 percent over twenty years, fixed. I knew we'd never get a better rate than that, so naturally we jumped on it. We even added some extra money to cover our build-out of the bottom floor. We were comfortable doing that because we would be leasing the second floor. The rent from that space would go toward paying our mortgage. When I amortized the cost again, I found that the mortgage payment was only $500 more per month than our current rent, and we were quadrupling the size of our facilities. The only downside during this busy time was having to miss the International Society for the Prevention of Perinatal and Infant Death (ISPID) conference in Amsterdam, where I was named the Educator of the Year. It still saddens me that I had to miss receiving that honor in person, but anyone who has ever bought and renovated property knows how all-consuming the process can be.

While we were negotiating the sale of the building, we heard that Graco's East Coast distributor—who dealt not only in Pack 'n Plays but also in car seats, baby swings, and high chairs—had gone out of business. We called our Graco representative, David Sternlieb, with an eye to expanding our services. Of course, his first reaction was that we'd never have the room to store enough inventory to make a go of it. When he heard we were buying a building with a fifteen-thousand-square-foot warehouse, he was ecstatic. Another hand-of-God moment—solving a problem for Graco and seizing an opportunity to expand our services and provide more discounted products to families in need.

Within four months of when Emily had first found the building, we'd bid on it, secured a mortgage, closed, and begun construction on our offices. The weeks leading up to the move were exhausting. Barb and I quickly realized that getting the building move-in ready would be a full-time job for us both. Luckily we had recently hired a warehouse manager, John Robinson, to lighten Barb's workload. In February HRSA had put out an RFP looking for a group to disseminate a consistent safe-sleep message throughout the country. Since we were already working on this through CAUSE, Teri Covington invited Judy Rainey, Stephanie Bryn (who had recently retired from HRSA), and me to East Lansing, Michigan, for a weekend to work with her and her colleague Linda Potter on a grant proposing that CDR and Cribs for Kids be jointly awarded the money. We stayed at Teri's house and worked out of her office. While we were there, her twenty-six-year-old son, John, was our savior. Each morning he made breakfast for us, and each afternoon he'd run to the office with our lunch. He did it all with a smile, chatting with us throughout the weekend, asking questions about our progress and our plans. On Sunday when we were getting ready to leave, I said, "John, it's a shame you don't live in Pittsburgh. I'm looking for someone to manage our warehouse. I have a feeling you'd be perfect."

He asked me some questions about how the warehouse was set up and what managing it would entail. I told him we were looking for someone to coordinate, train, and supervise our volunteers from Renewal so Barb could spend more time on the higher-level aspects of distribution.

"I would move to Pittsburgh for that job," he said. "If you're really offering it to me."

In addition to John, we added two other members to our team during that time period. Denise Puskaric works on shipping, invoicing, and the Managed Care Organization program which she breathed new life into through the development of an informational packet highlighting the innovative programming we offer. Brittany Johnson was accepted to medical school at St. George University, so we hired Tiffany Price as the new coordinator for our Hospital Certification Program. As applications come in from hospitals, Tiffany reviews them, sometimes after many telephone calls to Mike Goodstein and discussions with me, and assures they meet all the criteria for their applied-for designation.

With John and Denise taking on responsibilities in the warehouse, Barb was free to work with me on envisioning a design for the new office layout. Mike Moyta, a local architect, took our ideas and turned them into professional blueprints, promising a short turnaround time. Our next job was finding a contractor who would also work quickly. We had heard that building permits typically took eight to ten weeks to be issued. We were determined to find someone who could expedite the process for us. With Cribs for Kids growing so rapidly and our national conference looming, we couldn't spend months in flux between buildings.

As we were searching for a general contractor, a new tenant began construction at the North Shore office building. Their ten-thousand-square-foot renovation seemed to be progressing at lightning speed. I asked around and found out the contractor was T Construction, an all-woman company headed by Traci Yates. I met with her and asked her to submit a bid. Within two weeks of receiving the architect's drawings, her company had secured the building permits and started construction.

Until you've been through the process, you can't imagine the decisions and details that have to be addressed when you are remodeling sixty-five hundred square feet of office space: paint color, carpeting, countertop designs, appliances for break rooms and staging areas, cubicles, and furniture. We also had to coordinate Jeff Klingelhoefer, Rocco Favorite, and Lee Simmons to install our telephone and data lines—a far more daunting task than it was in the pre-Internet days. The logistics were mind-boggling to everyone, except Barb.

She shared plans for the individual offices with the staff members and had them measure their furniture and create room designs. She ordered the moving boxes and gave each of us a pallet in the warehouse where we could stack them so they'd be ready to be transported.

November 30, 2014, was move-in day. Dottie Coll, president of Two Men and a Truck's Pittsburgh operations, is one of our board members. I had met her when I spoke at a Chamber of Commerce meeting a few years earlier. She had been so enthralled with our story and Pitt Ohio Express' involvement that she insisted there must be something her company could do, too. We have a local outfit, Frank Fuhrer Distributing, that donates pallets to us to help keep down our shipping costs. Initially, we had to rent a truck to pick them up, which made the donation less attractive. This was the perfect fit, of course, for Two Men and a Truck, who now pick up the pallets from Fuhrer and deliver them to our warehouse.

Dottie generously donated two trucks and four workers to help us move to Hazelwood. Barb contacted Renewal and requested twelve volunteers to assist John and the movers. Moving two floors of offices and a warehouse is not typically a one-day task, but it turned out to be so, thanks to Barb's attention to detail and planning. She assigned the volunteers to either our North Shore location or our new building. Everyone worked together to load the trucks the first time. The Hazelwood crew rode to the new site to unload. Stickers had been placed on everyone's furniture so that it could be taken directly to the correct office and placed according to the diagram affixed to each door. The North Shore crew stayed behind and busily readied the items for the next truckloads and cleaned the empty offices. The day began at 8:00 a.m., and by 4:00 p.m. the volunteers, movers, John, Barb, and I sat down to enjoy pizza and soft drinks. True to our promise, the volunteers were back at Renewal by 5:00 p.m., tired but pleased that they had accomplished such a monumental task.

The next day a few of the volunteers were back, at our request, to help the employees carry their boxes to their offices. Jeff, Rocco, and Lee were also buzzing around installing our communication lines. By noon, we were up and running. Cribs for Kids was back in business.

Finding a tenant for the top floor was the final piece to the puzzle, as that rental income would pay our mortgage. Jeff Deitrick found us the perfect match in the Allegheny Intermediate Unit's Latino Family Center, which offers support services to families with children under age five. We are always looking to increase our outreach to Latino families. Now we have the perfect resource, right upstairs, to help us make those connections.

The final night of the conference when we hosted dinner at our offices, I found myself eating at a table with

Sam and Maura Hanke their dear friend and board member, Kate Menninger Desmond; Dick, and Jennie. Dick was asking them about Charlie's Kids.

"How did you first get involved with Cribs for Kids?" he asked Sam.

"We met at the AAP conference about four years ago," I answered for him.

Sam chuckled. "What you don't know is that we went to that conference just to meet you. We knew we had to get Cribs for Kids to distribute our book. I was so nervous talking to you. It was like meeting a rock star!" he said.

I don't tell you that to be boastful but because it was the second time someone had made a comment like that to me during one of our conferences, and it led me to a revelation. At the Welcome Reception at our previous conference, we gave Melissa Krall, one of the early adopters to our program, a Starfish Award for her work providing safe sleeping environments in Reno, Nevada. In her speech she talked modestly about her work and how much the recognition meant to her organization. As I listened to her speak admiringly about Cribs for Kids and the impact it has had on her, I realized that she—and so many others in the room— knew nothing of our early struggles, of the sleepless nights I spent agonizing about how much longer we could afford to keep our doors open. So many of them had become partners over the past few years when we were on our upward swing. They know us as a successful national organization with partners throughout the United States. I'm sure they couldn't imagine that not so long ago, we were rolling coins from canister fund raisers to cover the electric bill, or that when I started out, I was executive director of a two-person operation who jumped for joy if we raised a couple thousand dollars on a busy night at the gift-wrap booth.

I realized that if I could have one wish, it would be for all our partners to know our story—the lean times, the uncertainty, the feelings of desolation when we worried we couldn't help enough. I saw some of them going through similar struggles, and I wanted them to understand that those tough times wouldn't define them. They would also experience the aha moments, the times when everything clicks, the days when the hand of God reaches down and gives you a gentle shove in the right direction. We named the Starfish Award I mentioned in the previous paragraph after the parable about a young woman walking on the beach who finds hundreds of starfish washed up on shore. She is throwing them back in the water when a man walks by and says, "Why are you wasting your time? You'll never save them all. You can't make a difference." The girl picks one up and throws it into the water. "I made a difference to that one," she says. This story resonates with me because the truest thing I know is that all our efforts are meaningful. Every step we've taken, the clumsy stumbles *and* the exuberant leaps, have been part of the journey that got us to this place.

As the conversation continued around me, I sat back and reflected on how far we'd come. From having $2,000 in the bank to managing a $4.7 million budget. From working in two converted dorm rooms to owning a building and warehouse. From starting as a stand-alone organization to operating with more than six hundred fifty partners. From SIDS being called "unpredictable and unpreventable" to safe-sleep education driving down sleep-related death rates all over the country. From seven thousand babies dying per year to thirty-six hundred babies.

I excused myself and began to walk through the building, stopping to chat with guests along the way. I found myself showing off our workroom where volunteers assemble Safe Sleep Survival Kits; the warehouse where crews from Renewal palletize and shrink-wrap Pack 'n Plays and load and unload trucks; the kitchen where the staff meets throughout the day to talk over a cup of coffee or lunch.

Just as frequently, I stopped in empty spaces and talked about all the plans and visions we had for them. If I've learned anything along the way, it's that the most important parts of our new building are the parts that don't have a purpose yet—the uninhabited cubicles, the bare spots in the warehouse—because they are where inspiration dwells. Every day as I walk through the office, I imagine new ways to fill them.

If you are in need of infant safe-sleep products at discounted prices, please visit us at our online store.

ACKNOWLEDGMENTS

Five Ladies and a Forklift would not have been possible without the love, support, and talent of my daughter, Jennifer. As a middle-school language-arts teacher, Jennie's use of the English language and her creative-writing ability made this story informative, inspiring, and enjoyable to read. She was able to capture the unending perseverance of the "Five Ladies" because she was a part of the story from the beginning. Her ability to intertwine my personal story into a series of lessons created a treasure, not only for me but for readers who will be inspired to follow their passions and dreams.

Thank you to Judy Rainey, the third person on this writing team, for her dedication and commitment. Aside from providing editorial feedback, she was invaluable in adding another first-person perspective to many of the events and situations described.

As mentioned earlier, Dr. Eileen Tyrala's research was the basis for the chapter, "A Brief History of SIDS." I want to thank Eileen for not only compiling such an illuminating history but allowing us to draw from it here.

I want to extend my sincere appreciation to Dr. Michael Goodstein. He has been our champion since the beginning. As a member of the American Academy of Pediatrics' Task Force on SIDS, his passion and tireless devotion to spreading the word about infant safe sleep and Cribs for Kids have enabled us to expand from a local to a national organization with more than six hundred fifty partners throughout the country.

Because this book is a tribute to the Five Ladies and all of our employees, highlighting each of them and their contributions to Cribs for Kids, I don't feel it is necessary to again thank them individually for the success of our organization. I know they are aware of my eternal gratitude for furthering the cause of infant safe sleep and helping me on my journey. Although some board members were mentioned, I would like to thank all of our board members, past and present, who empowered me to follow my instincts. Their commitment to our ever-changing mission as we transitioned from SIDS of PA Inc. to Cribs for Kids Inc. has helped change a culture and save thousands of babies' lives in the process.

Cribs for Kids Board Members (2015–2016):

Chairman: Joseph T. Dominick, RN, MSN
Treasurer: Luci A. Casile
Secretary: Amy Berresford, CRNA, MS

James R. Agras
Erich Batra, MD, FAAP, FACP
Joan Braszo, LSW, CCM
Daniel Carlins
Dorothy Coll
Christopher Conti, MD
Noreen D. Crowell
Thomas Diecks
Joseph Fung
Molly Gaussa, JD
Michael Goodstein, MD, FAAP
Nalima Karamchandani, MD
Arnold Klein, JD
Deborah Kudravy, RN
Rev. Elwood Martin

Judy O'Connor
Richard Skorpenske
Todd Perrine
Dana Slizik

Of course, in addition to my daughter Jennifer, none of this could have been accomplished without the love, support, and hundreds of volunteer hours from my entire family—my husband, Dick; my son, Sean, and his wife, Lacey Horvat; my daughter, Kelly, and her husband, Michael James; and my grandson, Jack James, who became a Cribs for Kids volunteer when he was only five years old at our Breath of Life Stroll. Thanks for always showing up!